Other Books by Nathaniel Branden

The Six Pillars of Self-Esteem

The Art of Self-Discovery

The Power of Self-Esteem

Judgement Day

How to Raise Your Self-Esteem

To See What I See and Know What I Know

Honoring the Self

If You Could Hear What I Cannot Say

What Love Asks of Us

The Psychology of Romantic Love

The Disowned Self

Breaking Free

The Psychology of Self-Esteem

TAKING
Responsibility

Self-Reliance
and the
Accountable Life

Nathaniel
Branden

A FIRESIDE BOOK
Published by Simon & Schuster

FIRESIDE
Rockefeller Center
1230 Avenue of the Americas
New York, NY 10020

Copyright © 1996 by Nathaniel Branden, Ph.D.

First Fireside Edition 1997

FIRESIDE and colophon are registered
trademarks of Simon & Schuster Inc.

Designed by Elina D. Nudelman
Manufactured in the United States of America

10   9   8   7   6   5   4   3   2

Library of Congress Cataloging-in-Publication Data
Branden, Nathaniel.
    Taking responsibility : self-reliance and
the accountable life / Nathaniel Branden.
            p.   cm.
        Includes bibliographical references and index.
        1. Responsibility. 2. Self-reliance. I. Title.
BJ1451.B73   1996
158'.1—dc20   95-36640
                                                     CIP

ISBN 0-684-81083-2
        0-684-83248-8 (pbk)

Contents

Introduction

I will begin with a personal story that illuminates a primary aspect and benefit of self-responsibility that is rarely understood, the achievement of happiness.

As I approached my sixty-first birthday a few years ago, I found myself thinking a good deal about the subject of happiness, and about making its attainment my conscious purpose. At that time I was embarking on a project that had the potential to generate a good deal of stress, and I was determined that my daily mood and the harmony of my marriage not be adversely affected.

I thought about my wife Devers, who is the most consistently happy human being I have ever known, as well as one of the most self-sufficient. When I met her I felt that I had never encountered anyone for whom joy was more her "nature." Yet her life had not been easy. Widowed at twenty-four, she was left to raise two small children with very little money and no one to help her. When we met, she had been single for many years, had achieved success in a number of jobs, and never spoke of past struggles with any hint of self-pity. I saw her hit by disappointing experiences from time to time, saw her sad or muted for a few hours (rarely longer than a day), then saw her bounce back to her natural state of joy without any evidence of denial or repression. It took me some time to fully believe what I was seeing: that her happiness was *real*—and larger than any adversity.

When I would ask her about her resilience, she would say, "I'm *committed* to being happy." And she added, "That takes self-discipline." She also had a habit I thought unusual: She almost never went to sleep at night without taking time to review everything good in her life; those were typically her last thoughts of the day. I thought this was an important clue to what I wanted to understand about the psychology of happiness.

We talked about the fact that there is a tendency for most people to explain feelings of happiness or unhappiness in terms of the external circumstances of their lives. They explain happiness by pointing to the positives; they explain unhappiness by pointing to the negatives. The implication is that events *determine* whether they are happy; they take little or no responsibility for their state. I had always been convinced, as had Devers, that our own attitudes have far more to do with how happy we are than do any external circumstances.

I said to her: Take a man who is basically disposed to be happy, meaning that he feels happiness is his natural condition, and is happy a significantly greater amount of the time than he is unhappy. Let some misfortune befall him—the loss of a job, or a marriage, or being hit by some physical disability—and for some time he will suffer. But check with him a few weeks or months or a year later (depending on the severity of the problem) and he will be happy again. In contrast, take a man who is basically disposed to be unhappy, who feels unhappiness is more natural than joy, and who is unhappy a significantly greater amount of the time than he is happy. Let something wonderful happen to him—getting a promotion, inheriting a lot of money, falling in love with an exciting woman who returns his feelings—and for a while he will be happy. But check with him a little later down the line and very likely he will be unhappy again. We talked about research we had read that substantiated these observations.*

I have always considered myself an essentially happy person and have managed to stay happy under some fairly difficult circumstances. However, I have known periods of struggle and suffering, as we all have, and at times over the years I felt there was some error I was making and that not all of the pain was necessary. But what was I failing to grasp? That question preoccupied me now that I had decided to make happiness not merely a desire but a conscious purpose, to take a more proactive role in achieving the emotional state I wanted.

I thought of something I had noticed about myself. I sometimes joked that with each decade my childhood seemed to get happier. If you asked me at twenty or at sixty to describe my early years, the report would not have been different in its key facts, but in its emphasis. At twenty, the negatives in my childhood were in the front of my mind, so to speak, and the positives were at the back; at sixty, the reverse was true. As I grew older, my perspective and sense of what was important about those early years changed. This was another clue.

The more I reflected on these issues, and studied and thought about the happy individuals I encountered, the more clear it became that happy people process their experiences differently than unhappy people do. Happy people process their experiences so that, as quickly as possible, positives are held brightly in the foreground of consciousness and negatives are held dimly in the background. This is essential to understanding them.

But then I was stopped by the thought that none of these ideas and observations is entirely new to me and that at some

---

*See, for example, D. G. Myers' *The Pursuit of Happiness*.

level they are familiar. Why, then, have I not implemented them better throughout my life? Once asked, I knew the answer: Somehow long ago I had decided that if I did not spend a significant amount of time focused on the negatives in my life—the disappointments and setbacks—I was being evasive, irresponsible toward reality, insufficiently *serious* about my life. Expressing this belief in words for the first time, I saw how absurd it was. It would be reasonable *only if there were corrective actions I could be taking that I was avoiding taking.* But if I was taking every possible action, then a further focus on negatives *had no merit at all.*

If something is wrong, the question to ask ourselves is: Are there actions I can take to improve or correct the situation? If there are, I will take them. If there aren't, I do my best not to torment myself about what is beyond my control. Admittedly, this last task is not always easy, but it can be learned if one is determined.

The past several years, since making these identifications, have been the most consistently happy I have ever known, even though there were plenty of things about which to be agitated. I find that I deal with problems more quickly than I did in the past and that I recover more quickly from disappointments. I take more responsibility for my emotional state than I did when I was younger. Doing so does not feel like an onerous new task but like an experience of enhanced power—and liberation.

One of the ways I have learned to implement this policy, which I now teach to my therapy clients, is by beginning each day with two questions: *What's good in my life?* and *What needs to be done?* The first question keeps us focused on the positives. The second reminds us that our life and well-being are our own responsibility and keeps us proactive.

The world has rarely treated happiness as a state worthy of serious respect. And yet if we see someone who, in spite of life's adversities, is happy a good deal of the time, we should recognize that we are looking at a spiritual achievement—and one worth aspiring to. If we wish to achieve such happiness, and not merely wait for events or other people to make us happy, we need to grasp how intimately happiness is tied to self-responsibility and specifically, in this case, to taking responsibility for our emotions.

I begin with this story because the basic theme of this book is the liberating power of self-responsibility as a daily practice and orientation that we must grow into if we are to lead satisfying lives.

One characteristic of children is that they are almost entirely dependent on others. They look to others for the fulfillment of most of their needs. As they mature, they increasingly rely on their own efforts. One characteristic of successfully evolved adults is that they learn to take responsibility for their own lives—physically, emotionally, intellectually, and spiritually. We think of this as the virtue of independence or self-reliance. As an ideal of healthy development, it is basic to the American tradition of individualism.

But what such an ideal means precisely is not self-evident. We are social beings. The realization of our human potential can take place only in society. The participation and cooperation of others play crucially important roles in the meeting of most of our needs and in the attainment of almost all of our goals. Over 90 percent of us who work for a living do so in organizations, and the ability to function effectively as a member of a team is usually an imperative of success. On the more personal level, most of us do not seek a life of isolation. We choose to marry (and remarry) or share our lives with companions. Studies of happy people suggest the importance of a gratifying relationship with at least one other human being. The desire to experience some sense of community seems universal.

What then does it mean to speak of the virtue of self-reliance? What does it mean to celebrate the value of individualism? What does it mean to uphold the practice of self-responsibility?

These are the questions this book addresses.

In today's information economy, in which mind-work has so largely replaced muscle-work, in which authoritarian, hierarchical structures are giving way to more open, communicative structures, and in which cognitive skills are of paramount importance for successful adaptation to a rapidly changing global marketplace, the issue of self-responsibility has acquired a new urgency. Passive compliance has less and less economic utility. What business organizations need today are people who are willing and able to *think*—to be self-directing and self-managing—to respond to problems proactively rather than merely wait for someone else's solutions—to be *initiators*—to be, in a word, self-responsible.

In a world in which we are exposed to more information, more options, more philosophies, and more perspectives than ever before in our history, in which we must *choose* the values by which we will live our life (rather that unquestioningly follow some tradition for no better reason than that our parents did), we need to be willing to stand on our own judgment and trust our own intelligence—to look at the world through our own eyes—to chart our life-course and *think through* how to achieve the future we want—to commit ourselves to continuous questioning and learning—to be, in a word, self-responsible.

Let me caution against one common misunderstanding at the outset. Too often the idea of self-responsibility is interpreted to mean the taking on of new weights and obligations. It is equated with drudgery. Yet operating self-responsibly may entail saying no to burdens one never should have accepted in the first place. Many people find it easier to say yes to unreasonable requests than to stand up for their own interests. Taking on responsibilities that properly belong to someone else means behaving irresponsibly toward oneself. All of us need to know where we end and someone else begins; we need to understand *boundaries*. We need to know what is and is not up to us, what is and is not within our control, and what is and is not our responsibility.

In coming to understand what self-responsibility and independence mean and do not mean, we see that they are essential to personal fulfillment, basic to a moral life, and the foundation of social cooperation. We see that the conventional tendency to cast individualism as the enemy of community and culture rests on a profound misunderstanding.

Independence and self-responsibility are indispensable to psychological well-being. The essence of independence is the practice of thinking for oneself and reflecting critically on the values and beliefs offered by others—of living by one's own mind. The essence of self-responsibility is the practice of making oneself the cause of the effects one wants, as contrasted with a policy of hoping or demanding that someone else "do something" while one's own contribution is to wait and suffer. It is through independence and self-responsibility that we attain personal power. It is through the opposite that we relinquish our power.

In his book of the same title, Charles J. Sykes argues persuasively that we have become "a nation of victims." Clearly this syndrome is related to the diminished respect for self-responsibility in our culture. "I couldn't help it!" seems to be the most popular theme song of our day. It echoes the pronouncement of many of our social scientists that no one can help anything. Apart from the fact that this assertion cannot be substantiated and is false, it generates social consequences of incalculable harm. The abandonment of personal accountability makes self-esteem, as well as decent and benevolent social relationships, impossible. In its worst manifestation, it becomes a license to kill. If we are to have a world that works, we need a culture of accountability. It is toward that end that I write this book.

Opponents of accountability, professing to be humanitarians, often insist that people are sometimes hit by adversities beyond their control. True enough. But when people are down, they are better helped when they are awakened to the resources they do possess than when they are told they have none. The latter approach often masks condescension and contempt as compassion, whether practiced by a university professor, parent, spouse, legislator, or social activist. It is far easier to proclaim a concern for others than to think through what is most likely to be productive.

To tell a young criminal, for example, that when he robs a grocery store and brutalizes the owner, he is not really the guilty party—that the guilt belongs to the "system" that "oppresses" him—is morally corrupting both for the criminal and for the society in which he lives. To tell an unwed mother of sixteen about to have her second child that she is a helpless victim of patriarchy or capitalism and that state help is not charity but her rightful due, that she is entitled to food and shelter and medical care provided by what-does-it-matter-by-whom?—she is *entitled*—is morally corrupting and psychologically disempowering.

As a practicing psychotherapist, I regard my primary task as assisting people to access strengths they may not know they possess or do not know how to access so they may cope more effectively with the challenges of life. Whatever grief or anger they may first have to work through, the question they must ultimately confront is: Now what am I going to do? What options—what possibilities of action—exist for me? How can I improve the quality of my life? And to meet these questions, we have to discover that we are more than our problems. Our interests are not served when as adults, we see ourselves as helpless victims, even though we might have been as children.

Note that my advocacy of self-responsibility is very different from that of the conservative traditionalist or religionist who complains that there is "too much individualism" in our culture and that people need to learn greater self-responsibility out of duty to society (and/or to "God.") I am an advocate of individualism. I am also an advocate of an ethics of rational or enlightened self-interest. And it is because of that moral philosophy that I champion the practice of self-responsibility. To live responsibly is an act of intelligence and integrity, not of self-sacrifice.

In my past writing I dealt with self-responsibility exclusively as a source of self-esteem. In this book the focus is wider. Self-responsibility is shown to be the key to personal effectiveness in virtually every sphere of life—from working on one's marriage to pursuing a career to developing into an increasingly whole and balanced human being. It is both a psychological and an ethical principle. It constitutes the moral foundation of social existence and therefore has political ramifications as well.

Self-responsibility, independence, and autonomy are words to which some people respond with antagonism. Many people and groups today embrace the psychology of helplessness and victimhood and prefer to explain all their difficulties and struggles in terms of the actions of others. Given the amount of cruelty and injustice in the world, this preference is easy enough to rationalize. But there is also in our culture a countervailing tendency—a growing appreciation of the importance of self-reliance and of the need to take our destiny into our own hands. One evidence for this is the change in recent decades in the values parents are most eager to instill in their children.

In the nineteen-twenties a well-known study was conducted to identify the traits that parents in this country most prized in their children. The list was topped by traits associated with conformity and with dependence. Ranked highest were "loyalty to the church," "strict obedience," and "good manners." Traits associated with autonomy, such as "independence" and "tolerance," were rated low on the scale. Surveys conducted during the sixties, seventies, and eighties, however, increasingly reflect a radical shift of priorities—a reversal, in fact. Today parents most wish to see traits linked to autonomy in their children, such as "good sense," "sound judgment," "being independent," and "being tolerant," or comfortable dealing with people of other races and cultures. In contrast, "loyalty to the church," "strict obedience," and "good manners" have greatly diminished in popularity; they are now the preferred values of no more than 25 percent of those surveyed. This growing esteem for autonomy is found among white-collar and blue-collar families alike. And it is not confined to this country. A similar trend has been identified in Germany, Italy, England, and Japan.*

We are a long way from fully understanding and accepting the practice of self-responsibility as a way of life, with everything it entails personally and socially. To many people, some of what it entails may be not only challenging but disturbing— or worse. But there are stirrings of awareness. It just may be that self-responsibility is an idea whose time has come.

In this book I have four goals: to illuminate the meaning and implications of self-responsibility as a way of living and of being in the world; to show that this practice is not an onerous burden but a source of joy and personal power; to establish that we create our selves, shape our identity, through what we are willing to take responsibility for; and to demonstrate that self-responsibility, as well as self-reliance and individualism are essential to the well-being of our society.

On a more personal note, my hope for the reader is that he or she will find in this book a path to expanded awareness, heightened energy, greater personal effectiveness, and a wider vision of life's possibilities.

---

*"From Obedience to Independence," by Anne Remley. *Psychology Today*, October 1988.

1

Toward Autonomy

The most exciting event I can remember from the tenth year of my life was getting my first pair of *serious* long pants. They were dark blue and almost formal, not at all what a child would wear. They were meant for special occasions only, but I recall many times putting them on and walking up and down our street, admiring myself and wanting others to appreciate how distant I was from childhood. They were, I imagined, pants that might be worn by a businessman, or a doctor, or a "man of the world" who supported himself, managed his own life, and was engaged in doing something important. In other words, a *man.*

A "man," I felt then, without the words to express it, was someone who was independent, knew what he wanted, was in charge of his life, and certainly did not live with his parents. Someone who paid his own way, whose work meant creativity and joy. Someone who was cheerfully self-responsible and self-reliant. I thought of these traits as romantic, even heroic. (I still do, except that I would not limit the vision to the male gender.) And my symbol for that glamour figure was my dark blue trousers.

They were the promise and advance glimpse of a future I felt was beckoning and pulling me forward, toward a life where I would choose all my goals, where I would be answerable to no one (I did not yet understand the complexities of marriage), and where I could be the most important thing I knew of: *independent.*

Children's lives were managed by others; grown-ups, I thought, managed their own lives. If someone asked me what I wanted most in the world, I would have answered, "To be a grown-up."

I do not recall ever thinking about it consciously, but I am sure I assumed all my contemporaries felt as I did and were as fully impatient to attain adulthood. Today I know that this was not necessarily true. I could not have realized then and did not fully discover until I began the practice of psychotherapy that many grown-ups long to be children and in fact have never ceased being children. They look to others to tell them what to do. In important respects, they long to be taken care of, to be spared the necessity of thought, effort, and responsibility.

I had assumed that development from childhood to adulthood happened naturally and more or less automatically. I did not know how much more complex the truth was. I did not know how many things could go wrong or how many hazards there were along the way.

Selves Struggling to Emerge

No one comes into this world independent, autonomous, or self-responsible. This state of being is a product of *development:* It represents an achievement. Indeed, as I have discussed in previous books, no one is born an individual. In the beginning we are raw material. An individual is what we become as a result of successful growth and development. Our psychological birth in the full sense happens much later than our biological birth: The process takes not minutes or hours but years.

The natural progression from infancy to adulthood is from dependence to independence, from external support to self-support, from non-responsibility to self-responsibility. This is a process of *individuation,* which means separating, emerging, becoming whole, and fully becoming an individual. There are many stages to this developmental progression and they are not always negotiated successfully.

In our path toward adulthood, the attainment of physical maturity is the easiest part and is usually attained without difficulty. Intellectual, psychological, and spiritual maturity are another matter. At any step the process can be interrupted, frustrated, blocked, or sidetracked, either by an environment that obstructs rather than supports our growth, such as a home life that subjects us to gross irrationality, unpredictability, violence, and fear, or by choices and decisions that we make that are intended to be adaptive but turn out to be self-destructive. Such a choice, for instance, would be to deny and disown perceptions and feelings so that, short-term, life is made more acceptable, although in the process we give up pieces of ourself. Then growth is thwarted, intelligence is subverted, and many of the self's riches are left deep in the psyche, unmined. Like a sculptor's emerging figure, most of us remain trapped in an unfinished state, our potential felt rather than seen.

I recall a twenty-six-year-old woman, Julia K., who came to me in a state of crisis because her husband had left her and she felt terrified at the prospect of working for a living. "What do I know about the marketplace?" she cried. "What skills do I have that anyone would pay money for?" She had never considered it necessary to learn how to take care of herself in the world; she had been raised to believe that that was what husbands were for. When Julia was growing up, no one had thought it necessary or desirable to stimulate her mind, ask her what she thought, encourage her independence, or foster her self-reliance; and she had lacked the will to fight through on her own. Until the age of nineteen, when she married, her parents had made all her important decisions; then her husband had taken over that responsibility. Emotionally, Julia felt herself to be a child, with a child's level of self-sufficiency. The prospect of making independent choices and decisions, even about the simplest, most mundane matters—let alone going out in search of a job—filled her with anxiety.

"My alimony is only for three years," she informed me. It was if she had said, "The doctors have given me only three years to live." The idea of taking care of herself seemed to be utterly alien to her. And yet it could not have been entirely alien, because something led her to ask, "Do you think I could learn to be a *grown-up?*"

In therapy she was invited to struggle with the questions, "Who am I? What do I think? What do I feel? What do I want? What am I willing to take responsibility for? How can I translate what I am learning into action?" It was through confronting these issues and moving through the terror they initially evoked that Julia slowly learned to create herself, to give birth to an adult self capable of supporting her own existence.

The choice to exercise consciousness, to think and look at the world through one's own eyes, is the basic act of self-responsibility. I recall a fifty-three-year-old man, Andrew M., saying to me, as an example of the kind of issue he wanted to work on in therapy, "I always took it for granted I would support the same political party as my parents. Everyone in our family, all our relatives, vote the straight party ticket and always have. I think it would feel funny to vote differently. The idea of it makes me anxious. But, you know, a friend took me to a lecture of yours, and afterwards I began to wonder, Why do I take my party affiliation as natural when I've never really thought about these issues in my whole life? Something you said hit me—what I've been calling 'thinking' has just been bouncing around other people's opinions inside my head. I've never taken responsibility for an independent judgment. Sometimes I feel like I don't quite exist."

There is nothing remarkable about Andrew's statement except its explicitness. Millions of voters identify with one political party or another because that's what their families do. If asked what political or philosophical principles, or what thought processes led them to their orientation, they would have great difficulty answering and might resent the question. And there are many people who, having almost never had an independent thought, feel they "don't quite exist." But some spark of independence—some sense of responsibility to his own life—flickered in Andrew and led him to question his passivity. "What I'd like to have," he said, "are some opinions of my own."

For Andrew, the struggle toward autonomy and self-responsibility entailed thinking about the ideas accepted and propounded by his family, learning to distinguish their voices from his own, paying attention to his feelings, bringing awareness to internal signals of every kind, and making an effort to understand what things he read in the newspaper or books or heard on television that exposed him to a variety of viewpoints, and in the end taking responsibility for answering the questions, "What do I know to be true? What do I value? What do I respect? What am I willing to stand up for?" It was through struggling with these questions, learning to discover and honor his own sight, that he discovered the meaning of independence. The process was formidable. Andrew's dread of isolation and aloneness was not overcome easily.

The practice of self-responsibility is both an expression of our successfully achieved adulthood—our individuation—and also a means of attaining it, of bringing ourselves more completely into reality, shaping identity, and transforming potentiality into actuality.

Who I am may be understood as a function of what I am willing to take responsibility for.

Individuation

The stages of our development can be tracked in terms of our increasing capacity for autonomous (self-directed, self-regulated) functioning.

Birth itself is the beginning of this process: We leave our first matrix, the supporting structure of the womb, and begin to exist as a separate entity. While we are physically separate, however, we do not yet experience ourselves as separate. There is no ego. Several months will pass before we fully grasp physical boundaries, before we know where our body ends and the external world (including the mothering figure), begins. As brain, nervous system, and body develop, we accomplish one of our earliest and most important development tasks—our first discovery of *self*.

The grasping of *separateness*, the ability to distinguish between self and not-self, is the base of all subsequent development. Students of infant and child psychology call the process of achieving this awareness *separation and individuation*. In this context *individuation* refers to the second and overlapping part of the process, when basic motor and cognitive skills, as well as a beginning sense of physical and personal identity, are acquired and lay the foundation for the child's autonomy, his or her capacity for inner direction and self-regulation.

However, challenges of separation and individuation are not confined to the early years of life. When a man hits a spiritual crisis in midlife and feels compelled to question the values and goals of a lifetime, to redefine how he sees himself and what he wants for the rest of his years, he is separating from his past in order to open to his future and, this, too, is a process of individuation. When a woman who has been married for many years is suddenly divorced or widowed, and has to confront the question of who she is now that she is no longer someone's wife, she has to create a new sense of identity and this, too, is a process of individuation. Whenever someone's decades-old conception of himself is shattered and a new, expanded self-concept emerges, this a process of individuation.

The pattern from infancy onward is always the same: We say good-bye to one level of development so as to say hello to another. Saying hello to childhood means saying good-bye to infancy; saying hello to adulthood means saying good-bye to adolescence; saying hello to a new marriage or a new career means saying good-bye to the old one. This is why growth is sometimes represented metaphorically as a series of deaths and rebirths, and why growth can be frightening: It flings us from the known toward the unknown.

Without going into the technicalities of developmental psychology, I need to say a few more words about how a mature human self emerges, so as to establish the place of autonomy and self-responsibility in the human story.

The self that develops in the first year of life is a *body-self.* If an infant could grasp and answer the question, "Who are you?"—the answer would be, "I am my body." This is where identity originates.

Boundaries are essential to the experience of selfhood, and the first and most basic boundary is physical. This fact may help us to understand why physical or sexual abuse can be so psychologically devastating. When a young person's body-boundary is violated, it undermines his or her sense of self.

An infant exists as a separate body before acquiring consciousness of an independent body-self. Similarly, a child has feelings and emotions before clearly recognizing them as aspects of his or her self—that is, before developing an *emotional-self.* The body-self typically develops between the fifth and ninth months; the emotional-self develops between the first and third years. Until both stages of development have been reached, an infant does not clearly differentiate its emotional-physiological experiences from those of its mother or anyone in the environment. Feelings and emotions exist but are not clearly differentiated, and there is no awareness of whose they are.

"I" no longer means only "my body"; now it means "my feelings and emotions and my body." It is interesting to note that among persons who are strongly disposed to form "codependent relationships," these boundaries have never been fully established, so that the feelings of others are sometimes treated as our own. Certainly "codependency," in which one's own identity is inappropriately intertwined with that of another at the expense of one's own well-being, reflects a failure of adequate individuation.

Between the third and sixth years the child learns to think and to recognize ownership of thoughts. The child learns to express feelings and wants verbally, to announce perceptions, to make (more advanced) connections and integrations, to make distinctions, and to use thoughts to regulate behavior. This is obviously a more advanced stage of autonomy. The child is now more of a *person*. A new sense of "I" forms that both includes and goes beyond what has been before. The child acquires a *mental-self*.

The child has shifted from "I am my body" to "I am my feelings and emotions and my body" to "I am my thoughts and also my feelings and emotions and body."

Notice that the experience of self keeps expanding. It contains earlier levels of self-awareness and goes beyond them. Selves *grow*. What concerns us here *is the direction in which they are growing—what they are growing toward.*

Each of the three stages I have mentioned plays an essential role in laying the foundation for a well-developed sense of identity. There are higher levels of development, to be sure, but when these three basic levels are not negotiated successfully pathology develops.

Briefly, students of development associate a failure of appropriate growth at stage one with psychosis (no clear, differentiated sense of self and reality); a failure at stage two with borderline disorders (weak emotional boundaries, overwhelming anxiety and depression); and a failure at stage three with neurosis (resulting from the disowning and repressing of "unacceptable" thoughts and feelings, and showing up in such classic "neurotic" symptoms as hypochondria, obsessive-compulsive behavior, irrational fears, and the like).

With the emergence of a mental-self, a child attains new powers. These include the ability to deny, disown, and repress thoughts, feelings, emotions, and memories that evoke anxiety: to cut off aspects of the self and to shrink the *experience* of self, so as to function with less distress. While the intention is to protect emotional equilibrium, such repression is self-constricting, diminishing, alienating, and growth-arresting.

One aspect of the individuation process later in life is the discovering, owning, and integrating of previously repressed material, thereby expanding the experience of self and strengthening self-esteem. A child can disown feelings of anger, lust, excitement, ambition, or any other agitating and "unacceptable" emotion, and then, years later, learn to reclaim these denied parts and to declare, "This, too, is part of me, or an expression of me," and thus to achieve a richer and more balanced sense of identity. To accept and integrate previously disowned or undiscovered aspects of self is basic to psychological growth and well-realized individuality. Not only emotions, but also thoughts, attitudes, talents, values, and other resources may need to be reclaimed; and as they are, more of who we are emerges from the rock of potentiality.

As we move along the path of individuation through childhood to adolescence, we grow in knowledge, skills, and the ability to process information. While not yet in possession of the self-reliance possible to an adult, by adolescence we have taken a big step beyond the dependency of our earlier years. We have grown in personal power. Our thinking is less tied to the immediate sensory environment. We have shifted from concrete, sense-bound thinking to increasingly abstract thinking. We are learning to think conceptually and in principles, grasping more and more complex relationships and building higher and higher structures of knowledge.

In step with this process, our sense of self keeps evolving. To the extent that our development is successful, our mind and its cognitive processes—thinking, understanding, learning—become our primary source of identity and security. *Self-reliance is reliance on one's consciousness—on one's power of awareness.*

This state is the culmination of a journey that began with separation from the womb and went on to separation from the mother and separation from and transcendence of one form of environmental support after another. Not that external supports do not play a role for adults; they do. But the climax of individuation is the shifting of the *primary* support from the external to the internal, from the environment to the self. In terms of survival and well-being, this occurs when we accept basic responsibility for our existence: when we learn to rely predominantly on our own thought and effort for the fulfillment of our needs and goals. In terms of self-esteem, it occurs when we and not others become the primary source of our approval.

A basic goal in therapy is to assist the client to move toward this state of being by shifting authority and power from the world to the self. A young man—Mark R.—consulted me because, having graduated college at the age of twenty-four, he was under enormous pressure to enter the family business. It was a company that manufactured leather goods, which his father had founded decades earlier and which provided employment for many uncles, aunts, and cousins, apart from other employees. Mark was regarded as the "brain" of the family, and it had long been his father's dream that one day his son would replace him as head of the company.

But Mark had a lifelong fascination with philosophy and dreamed of acquiring a Ph.D. and becoming a professor—a profession which his parents and other relatives found incomprehensible, unrelated to the "real world." He came to see me because he was torn between, on the one hand, his love for his family and his desire to retain their approval, and, on the other hand, his passion for work that would take him outside the sphere of his family's understanding. I pointed out that his conflict itself was philosophical because it entailed choosing among competing values; and also that it was psychological because what he was struggling with was less like an unsolved problem in logic than a choice between motivation by love versus motivation by fear. The love derived from the joy he associated with working in the field of philosophy; the fear derived from anxiety about losing the emotional support of his family.

"Nothing wrong with wanting your family's approval," I said, "but the question is, What price are you willing to pay to keep it?"

He answered, "I feel like what they want from me in exchange for their blessing is that I sacrifice my soul."

"And what," I went on, "do you imagine will be the consequences if you give them what they want?"

He whispered sadly, "I feel like the most valuable part of me will die. My self-esteem, yes, but more than that, more than my self-esteem—my fire and enthusiasm for life."

I remarked that when we surrender the first, we almost inevitably lose the second. "It doesn't sound like a profitable trade," I said.

In a later session Mark said to me, "I'm beginning to see that choosing the career path that feels right for me means standing totally and absolutely on my own judgment, living self-responsibly at a very deep level, not just financially, which is easy, but also *spiritually,* if you know what I mean."

If the basic meaning of "spiritual" is "pertaining to consciousness" (in contrast to "material," which means "pertaining to or constituted by matter"), then of course Mark was right. It *was* a spiritual battle in which he was engaged, having everything to do with individuation and autonomy.

In the end Mark decided in favor of his own career preference, and after a difficult year his family adjusted to his decision, although Mark felt that some element of closeness was irretrievably lost. "Maybe that's a necessary part of growing up," he said at our final session.

Thinking About Values

Moral or ethical values are principles that guide our actions in issues and matters open to our choice. If we did not have to make choices—if we couldn't pursue many different goals by many different means—we would not need a code of morality. If our life and well-being did not depend on our making choices that are appropriate both to reality and to our own nature, we would not have to deal with questions like: By what values should I live my life? By what principles should I act? What should I seek and what should I avoid?

Psychologists are far from united in their views of how the self as a moral agent evolves, but there is fairly strong agreement that successful culmination of this process calls for the individual to behave in ways he or she judges to be moral not out of fear of punishment or social disapproval or out of blind, conformist rule following, but out of an authentic, firsthand assessment of the right and wrong involved. Here again, then, we confront the issue of autonomy and individuation. Imitative rule following represents a fairly early stage of a child's development, to be outgrown and transcended with subsequent knowledge and authority.

However, as long as we think for ourselves about moral matters, we can find ourselves in conflict with the teachings of significant others in our world. Our own judgment might tell us to be compassionate when conventional morality says to be stern, or to be indignant when conventional morality says to be humble, or to be proud when conventional morality says to be self-disparaging, or to be challenging when conventional morality says to be compliant, or to be self-assertive when conventional morality says to be self-sacrificial. We might find ourselves clashing with people important to us about issues such as abortion, sexual practices, differing ideas about rights and responsibilities, government regulation of our lives, or any matters that involve our values. Then the question becomes: Will we remain loyal to our judgment or will we surrender it in order to "belong?" Will we preserve our autonomy or betray it?

Most of us admire people who have the courage and integrity to remain loyal to honest, reasoned convictions in the face of opposition and animosity. At some level, we *know* that independence is our proper state, whether or not we fully achieve it. Only an authoritarian personality is likely to dispute that it is better to think moral issues through autonomously than to make decisions based on habitual conformity or fear. We may wish to check our reasoning against the reasoning of others, for objectivity, but to the extent that we function autonomously we know that ultimate responsibility for our choices and decisions is ours alone. Autonomy entails self-responsibility.

Being Autonomous

Autonomy pertains to self-regulation: control and direction from within, rather than from any external authority.

Autonomy is expressed through an individual's capacity for independent survival (supporting and maintaining one's existence through productive work), independent thinking (looking at the world through one's own eyes), and independent judgment (honoring inner signals and values).

Autonomy should not be interpreted as self-sufficiency in the absolute sense. It does not mean that one lives on a desert island or should act as if one did. Nor should our focus on autonomy, independence, and individuation be construed as denial of the obvious fact that we constantly learn from others and clearly benefit from interactions with them. As I said at the outset, we are social beings. We speak a common language and influence and affect each other in countless ways. We need each other's participation to fulfill most of our goals. That we live in a social context is *assumed* in this discussion.

And yet consciousness by its nature is immutably private. We are each of us, in the last analysis, islands of consciousness. To be alive is to be an individual, and to be an individual who is conscious is to experience a unique perspective on the world. To be an individual who is not only conscious but self-conscious is to encounter, if only for brief moments in the privacy of one's own mind, the fact of our ultimate aloneness. No one can think for us, no one can feel for us, no one can live our life for us, and no one can give meaning to our existence except ourselves.

There are a thousand respects in which we are not alone. As human beings, we are linked to all other members of the human community. As living beings, we are linked to all other forms of life. As inhabitants of the universe, we are linked to everything that exists. We stand within an endless network of relationships. We are all parts of one universe. But within that universe, we are each of us a single point of consciousness, a unique event, a private, unrepeatable world.

It is precisely this fact that gives love its power and intensity, that allows merging to turn into ecstasy. However, no one is ready for love in the adult sense who has not made peace with the fact of his or her aloneness and accepted responsibility for his or her existence. Romantic love is for grown-ups.

More than one client in therapy has said to me, "One of the things that makes self-responsibility difficult is that it makes me feel so *alone*. It's frightening."

I typically reply, "You mean, it's frightening to accept that no one is coming. No one is coming to rescue you. No one is coming to spare you the necessity of thought and effort. It's hard sometimes really to let this in and absorb it. I do see that it's hard for you. And yet, you know, it's true: No one is coming. What are your ideas on how you might deal with this problem?"

Although we do not reflect on it consciously, when we exercise an independent process of thought or judgment, we implicitly connect with our aloneness. Thinking is not a social activity. When we recognize that we are the author of our choices and actions we experience our separateness. When we take the responsibility for our life and well-being proper to an adult human being, we underscore our individuation. To a self-confident mind this process is as natural and untroublesome as breathing. But if we have not grown to proper human adulthood, if we lack confidence in our competence and worth, this process may feel formidable and alarming and may become one of the reasons we dread self-responsibility. Then the challenge is to confront our fears and take whatever steps are necessary to graduate from childhood.

Otherwise, instead of feeling efficacious in the face of life's challenges, we are doomed to feel powerless.

Efficacy

"Efficacy" is the ability to produce a desired result. To be efficacious in the fundamental sense is to be able to cope with the challenges of life. We all desire—and need—this sense of competence. It is one of the core aspects of self-esteem.

Everyone has seen the delight of an infant banging a spoon against a table and producing a loud sound: The infant is affirming and reaffirming that he or she *can make something happen.* This is an experience of personal power, personal efficacy, and it is in our nature that, because of its obvious survival value, we will greet this experience with joy. At any age, when we feel efficacious we tend to feel that we are good and that life is good instead of feeling that we are helplessly ineffectual reactors in a malevolent universe.

We are born into a condition of total helplessness. Without the aid of others, we cannot feed or dress ourselves or even move across the room. Without caretakers we cannot survive. But from the beginning the direction of our learning and growth is normally toward independence and efficacy. As we develop, we learn to move by our own effort, to put food into our own mouth, to communicate with others through language, to select the clothes we will wear today, to walk to school on our own, to read, to master arithmetic and later mathematics, to drive an automobile, to understand increasingly complex subjects such as physics and literature, to move into our own apartment, to form a philosophy of life, to enter into contracts with other people, to engage in productive work—in brief, to become self-supporting and self-responsible. The track of individuation is also the track of increasing competence or increasing efficacy. Looking back over our life, any of us can see the many ways growth equates higher stages of mastery, and the intimate relationship between efficacy and becoming more fully our own person.

In the nineteen-thirties an idea about child-rearing gained wide currency but had unfortunate results for the children of parents who accepted it. This was the belief that children should be picked up, hugged, fed, and otherwise cared for according to a schedule entirely determined by adults. It was taught that children should not be attended to merely because they cried or shouted or waved their arms. Apart from seeing that the child was not in pain, parents were advised to ignore such signals, so children would not be "spoilt." Later it was observed that children raised in this manner tended to lack social competence; they tended not to interact well with other children or with adults; they were often passive socially. They had not learned that through their own actions they could produce a desired effect on other human beings. They did not experience themselves as the cause of any parental behavior. They did not have an opportunity to experience this form of efficacy. Consequently, as they grew, they faced other human beings without the confidence that comes from experiencing some sense of power. To develop appropriately, then, we need the experience of having wants and learning what actions we can take to satisfy them.

A child wants to move across the room and acquires the skill to do so. A child wants to communicate thoughts and feelings and acquires the necessary language skills. A child wants to ride a bicycle and learns how to do it. A child's *wants* constitute one of the most important driving forces of growth. We are pulled along the path of our development not only by the maturation of body and brain but also by the values that energize us—*that we take responsibility for achieving.*

A therapy client once wondered aloud why he had not become more independent as an adult. I asked if he had ever made independence a goal or purpose and he had answered no. Perhaps that explained it, I suggested.

If efficacy pertains to our ability to satisfy our needs and achieve our goals, then clearly it is a necessity of well-being. What I want to stress is that individuation is inseparable from the growth of efficacy—that is, from learning how to think, acquire skills, master challenges, cope with new and unfamiliar situations, and extend the range of competence. What we are able to do is intrinsic to the experience of who we are. Through learning, I continue the process of creating myself—not just in childhood but across a lifetime.

Self-Responsibility

As we grow in efficacy, as we become more competent to cope with the challenges of life, we find self-responsibility easier and more natural to practice. And as we practice self-responsibility, we grow in efficacy. The relationship is reciprocal.

Thinking about self-responsibility, I am reminded of an old joke. A wealthy lady exits from a stretch limousine and then her young son, who looks to be about ten, is borne out on a pillow carried by four servants. A bystander says to the woman, "Oh, madam, your poor son! Can't he walk?" And the woman answers haughtily, "Of course he can walk. But thank God he doesn't have to."

In real life, no one is entirely lacking in self-responsibility. If we did not initiate some actions on our own behalf, we could not exist. Even the most passive and dependent of us is self-responsible in some areas some of the time. That is, we all accept the task of being the cause of some desired effects.

One of the natural pleasures of childhood is the discovery "I can do it!" When accomplishments are treated by adults not as duties but as signs of growth and maturation, children can be heard exclaiming proudly, "I can tie my shoes!" "I can help clear the table!" "I'll get the rake, Daddy!" "I can recite the whole alphabet!" "I can read that sign!" "I can make my own lunch!" In these examples we can see how closely self-responsibility and efficacy are related. It is as if, at the start of life, nature gives us a push in the right direction by linking these experiences with enjoyment, satisfaction, and pride. But we do not continue moving in that direction effortlessly or automatically.

If, as children grow, all choices and decision are made for them by adults, if no expectations are held up to them and no responsibilities required, the danger is that they will remain dependent, inadequately individuated, underdeveloped in competencies appropriate to their age, and of course not self-responsible. If too much is expected of children too soon, if they are burdened by demands beyond their capacity, the danger is that they will sink into passivity and feelings of defeat and congenital incompetence and, again, will not properly individuate or learn self-responsibility.

If parents understand that by the design of our natures we are intended to evolve toward autonomy, and if they choose to support and align themselves with this process, then they will want to be sensitive to opportunities for nurturing competence and self-responsibility. They will seek to elicit not obedience but cooperation. They will look for ways to stimulate thinking. They will teach their children to appreciate causal connections between actions and consequences. They will create an environment of safety, respect, acceptance, and trust, in which a healthy self can grow. They will look for opportunities to offer their children age-appropriate choices and responsibilities and thus teach accountability. They will assign tasks that allow the child to make some contribution to the running of the household, such as clearing the table, emptying the garbage, or cutting the lawn, so that the child gains experience in feeling effective as a family member. They will teach (and model) the virtue of perseverance. They will celebrate achievements. They will honor signs of self-responsibility. They will communicate their belief in the child's abilities and worth.

The Meaning of Maturity

There is in almost everyone some implicit awareness of the fact that the natural expression of proper adulthood is self-responsibility. One of the ways this is evidenced is our tendency to describe certain behavior as "childish."

For example, if a couple has had a conflict and each is sulking and waiting passively for the other to do something, we say that their behavior is childish because they are avoiding taking any responsibility for achieving a resolution. If a woman continues to let her mother make all her important decisions, even though the woman is now in her twenties, we say that "she's still a child" because she takes so little responsibility for her life. If a man refuses to be accountable for his actions and is always engaged in blaming or using alibis, we say, "He's never grown up"—because one of the traits we identify with adulthood is willingness to be responsible for what one does. If a woman blindly and trustingly turns over the management of her inherited money to a stranger about whom she knows nothing, and the money vanishes, and the woman wails, "Why me?" we say, "She acted like a five-year-old," because we expect an adult to be more responsible about her choices. If we see that a man is afraid to offer an opinion about any subject without first knowing what his authority figures believe, we consider this as evidence of immaturity, because we identify maturity with some measure of independent thinking and thus self-responsibility. If we see a woman dominated by a hunger for compliments and attention, yet unable to carry her own weight in any relationship, unable to give any of the values she expects from others, we say, "She's as self-absorbed as an infant," because for infants dependence and neediness are a natural state. Or, to offer a different kind of example, if we say that paternalistic governments "infantalize" people, we mean that such governments undermine and penalize self-responsibility and reward the opposite. The point is, we do not associate self-responsibility with two-year-olds; we associate it with grown-ups.

Questions

Many factors contribute to the course of our development. One is our biological inheritance. Another may be the birth experience itself. Another is the nature of our interactions with other human beings as we are growing up. Another factor—and the one most often ignored—is *the creative role that we ourselves play.*

We are not merely passive clay on which biology, external events, and other people write. No attempt to explain an individual by reference only to biological and environmental elements has ever succeeded: There is always the unpredictable, mysterious contribution of the person involved. We are active contestants in the drama of our lives. We have choices, and our choices matter. This is a central theme in my previous book, *The Six Pillars of Self-Esteem.*

In Chapter 2 we will examine the issue of choice and responsibility in more detail, but it can hardly be denied that if we *expect* ourselves to operate self-responsibly, and if others expect it of us, we are more likely to do so than if it isn't expected. If our personal philosophy *values* autonomy, and if the culture does also, we are more likely to evolve toward it than if conformity is prized instead. If we *want* to grow up, and if our social milieu respects rather than scorns such "adult" values as productive work, a capacity for deferred gratification, and the ability to think and plan long-range, then the chances are that we will attain some measure of maturity. Otherwise, chances are that we will march toward old age without ever graduating from childhood or adolescence. The point, simply, is that self-responsibility, autonomy, and maturity are most likely to be attained when they are adopted as *values* and chosen as *goals*.

Our values and goals provide the motive power and the direction for our development. We shape our identity and advance our efficacy *through what we are willing to take responsibility for.*

Although we have spelled out the meaning of self-responsibility in a general way, when we reflect on it we see that the idea requires some unpacking. For example, if I say I take responsibility for my actions, what exactly do I mean? If I say I take responsibility for my choices and decisions, what is it I want you to understand? If I say I take responsibility for the level of consciousness I bring to my activities, or for my choice of companions, or for the way I deal with people, or for the values I live by, or for the level of my self-esteem, or for the way I treat my body, or for my spiritual development, what do such declarations *mean*? Am I saying that I claim absolutely no control over my life? Or that I deny the reality of external influences? Or that I am never affected by factors beyond my control? Or that for all practical purposes I operate in a vacuum and that other people are not essential to my fulfillment? These are all questions we will need to consider.

There is no question that self-responsibility and the ability to make choices are intimately related. The concept of self-responsibility presupposes free will. In contrast, apostles of non-responsibility deny any form of psychological freedom and assert that our beliefs, actions, and values are all determined by factors outside our control, by our biology and "conditioning." What is involved in this conflict?

2

Freedom and Responsibility

The
practice of self-responsibility begins with the recognition that
I am ultimately responsible for my own existence; that no one
else is here on earth to serve me, take care of me, or fill my
needs; I am the owner of no one's life but my own. This means
that I am willing to generate the causes of the effects I want. It
also means that if I need the cooperation of others in the pursuit of my goals, I must provide them with reasons meaningful
in terms of their own interests and needs; my wants per se are
not a claim on anyone.

Furthermore, as I live my life, I have the choice to operate
mindfully or mindlessly or anywhere between. I am accountable in any issue for the level of awareness I select. To think is
an act of choice; so is to avoid thinking, and I am the cause of
that choice. Self-responsibility entails my willingness to be accountable for my choices, decisions, and behavior. I take responsibility for thinking about the consequences of my actions
and hold myself accountable for them as well. When I choose
an action whose consequences I can foresee, I am also choos-

ing the consequences, and I accept that fact.

I am responsible for how I deal with other people: spouse, children, colleagues, associates. If I behave destructively toward them, I don't claim that they or anyone else "made me do it." I do not give away my power or delude myself that others have power over me in ways they demonstrably do not.

Practiced consistently, self-responsibility implies my willingness to be accountable for the ideas and values by which I conduct my life. This entails intellectual independence: the willingness to think for myself and act by the judgment of my own mind. I learn from others, to be sure, but I do not grant to others authority over my consciousness or follow blindly where I do not understand or agree. I do not live secondhand.

If I accept the principle of self-responsibility I recognize that the achievement of my happiness is no one's task but my own. No one owes me happiness. In a love relationship I want the opportunity to *share* my happiness, not find someone who will "make" me happy.

Just as no one can make me happy, no one can give me self-esteem. That, too, is my responsibility.

In sum, I am responsible for my life, well-being, and actions *in all those areas and issues open to my choice.*

What My Responsibility Is and Is Not

Just as I need to know what I am responsible for, I also need to know what I am not responsible for. I need to know what is within my power and what is not within my power. I need to know my limits, which is to say only that I need to know my identity.

I am responsible for my choices and actions, but for no one else's. I can influence but I cannot control another mind. I cannot determine what someone else will think or feel or do.

If I hold myself responsible for matters beyond my control, I will put my self-esteem in jeopardy, since inevitably I will fail my expectations. If I deny responsibility for matters that are within my control, again I will jeopardize self-esteem. Knowing what is and what is not up to me is an issue of the highest importance.

I am thinking of a client I once worked with, Marge L., an excellent manager who took a keen interest in the development of her staff and did everything she could to inspire and bring out the best in them. There was one young woman in whom she saw immense potential, except that this young woman had a predilection for disastrous love affairs that tended to distract from and undermine her work. Marge made the effort she could to help her and gave her extra time, attention, and training, but to no avail. When she was forced to let the young woman go, she felt guilty and reproached herself for not finding a way "somehow" to save her. If she were a really good manager, she told herself, this failure would not have happened. Because Marge did not recognize her limits, which included being neither infallible nor omniscient, she placed her self-esteem at the mercy of other people and allowed their choices to dictate her sense of worth.

One often sees this pattern develop between parents and children. Sometimes parents torture themselves because, even though they have done their conscientious best, their children do not develop as the parents hoped. And the parents feel guilt. By implication, they imagine themselves to possess a power no one possesses: the power to determine the choices another human being will make. If individuation is an issue for children it is also an issue for parents. Both need to achieve appropriate separation. Both need to learn where self ends and the other begins.

Sometimes one sees this pattern between husbands and wives. A wife despairs because in spite of her best efforts she cannot stop her husband's drinking. Or a husband despairs because no matter what he does he cannot stop his wife's attachment to tranquilizers. If only I knew the right thing to say or do, they may tell themselves, as if total power could be theirs if only they knew how to tap into it. They may believe in their own free will, but they do not believe in their partner's. They do not accept the boundaries that separate one human being from another.

If we must learn that we do not have control over the minds and lives of others, we also must learn that our control over our own life is not unlimited either. Free will does not mean omnipotence. It is a force in our lives, to be sure, but it is not the only force. All of us are affected at times by forces—political, economic, environmental, or genetic—that we clearly do not choose. We have options about how we will respond to those forces but not about their existence or the fact that they have *some* impact. A simple example: In bad times we may have no choice about the fact that our employer lays us off, but we usually have several choices about what we do next—hunt for another job, use the time off to acquire some new skill, try to start a business of one's own, surrender to despair and get drunk, to name only a few. Viktor Frankl's *Man's Search for Meaning* discloses the options that exist even in a Nazi concentration camp and the forms of spiritual heroism of which humans are capable.

Just the same, I want to emphasize that terrible things do happen to innocent people. Individuals do suffer through no fault of their own. And sometimes their options are severely limited.

This must to be stressed because some alleged enthusiasts for responsibility come close to giving the idea a bad name, by the grandiosity of their claims. "I am responsible for everything I experience," they proclaim. "I create my own reality." I remember asking on more than occasion if this meant that a baby napalmed in a war zone is responsible for the experience; the answer was always the same: an unhesitating *yes*. Just as money diminishes in value as the currency is inflated, so the idea of responsibility diminishes in significance as more and more extravagant claims are made on its behalf. I believe that the purpose of grandiose notions of responsibility is compensation for core feelings of powerlessness, of impotence dreaming of unlimited control over the universe. In terms of real effectiveness in a real world, there is more efficacy in understanding that "nature, to be commanded, must be obeyed," than in telling oneself, "I create my own reality." But it is an efficacy that comes from recognizing facts, identity, and limits. (We may have to challenge false notions of what our limits are, and that is a different matter.) Contrary to claims one sometimes hears today, it is not true that one can have unlimited power or be a "no-limit person" or that "anything we believe is possible, *is* possible." People have died from "believing" that the bridge ahead was not washed away by the flood, or by "believing" that their next injection of heroin was safe, or by "believing" (while on LSD) that they could fly. If the idea of responsibility is to be meaningful, it must be based in reality and not in fantasy.

Finally, I want to emphasize that the sense of responsibility I use in this context carries no necessary implication of guilt or moral blame. I write of responsibility as *causal agency,* as in "I am the cause of my choices, decisions, and actions—I am responsible for them." (In Aristotle's formulation: "The principle of motion is within.") Whether blame is appropriate in any particular case is a different question entirely. "Responsibility" per se is a morally neutral term.

Free Will and the Choice to Operate Consciously

Self-responsibility implies free will—that is, a sphere in which freedom of choice exists. Self-responsibility presupposes volition.

I have examined the nature of free will and the contradictions of determinism at some length in earlier books of mine, in particular *The Psychology of Self-Esteem* and *Honoring the Self.* So I will confine the present discussion to a few essentials.

Our basic psychological freedom is the power to regulate the action of our consciousness. It is the choice to seek awareness or not to bother or actively to avoid awareness. When faced with facts requiring our attention, we can choose to focus our mind and brighten the searchlight of our awareness, or we can choose to remain passive and see only that which comes to us easily and without effort, or we can run from even a modest level of awareness, as if to obliterate reality by refusing to see it.

No special subtlety of observation is needed to make us aware of these options. We encounter them every moment of our waking existence.

In any given situation, we have choices concerning the level of consciousness we activate. We can give full attention, half-attention, zero-attention, or anywhere in between. Whatever the choice, we are its cause. This is the essence of our free will.

In what forms might this issue confront us in everyday life? Here are some examples.

- My spouse is talking to me, seeking my understanding of some hurt or grievance. Do I listen with a genuine desire to understand? Or with my mind half on my work? Or am I more focused on preparing my defense than on grasping her point?

- My boss is giving instructions. Is my attention on what he or she is saying, or do I choose to remain in a haze of boredom and resentment because mental effort feels like an imposition?

- I meet a person to whom I am romantically attracted. I feel we might be soul mates. At the same time, I note behaviors that clash with my best vision of this person and that disturb me when I think about them. Do I raise the level of my awareness at this point or do I lower it?

- While driving my car, I am steaming with anger over an argument I had with my teenage son or daughter. Do I stay focused on my primary responsibility in the moment, which is the safe operation of my automobile, or am I am recklessly unconcerned with what I am doing, so caught up am I in ruminations about the argument?

- I am a physician, and my female patient is describing her symptoms. For reasons I have never chosen to examine, I tend to be impatient with women and often tend to tune them out. Do I consider her story conscientiously, or do I reflexively prescribe Valium?

- I am the CEO of a company that has been losing income and market share for the past several years. Do I look at the evidence that policies that worked in the past are nonresponsive to current market realities? Or do I shut off my mind and keep muttering, "Things have got to get better"?

- I hear new arguments against my political views that I had never considered before and that leave me somewhat agitated. Do I reflect on those arguments to the best of my rational ability, or do I blank them out so as to avoid the effort of thought and, possibly, the need to change some premises?

In all such cases, I make choices involving the operation of my consciousness, choices about thinking or non-thinking. I am the cause of those choices and I am responsible for them. I am also responsible for the actions I subsequently take—with my spouse, job, automobile, patient, company, or political action group—that reflect my thinking or nonthinking.

I am responsible for the level of consciousness I bring to my work, to my relationships, to any activity in which I engage. The practice of self-responsibility—or its avoidance—begins here. The essential point to understand for our purposes is that while mind is our basic tool of survival, its exercise is not automatic: It requires an act of choice. We can seek to understand, or we can seek to avoid understanding. We can respect facts, or we can pretend they do not exist. We can operate rationally or irrationally, mindfully or mindlessly. We can open our eyes or close them.

We are the one species that can formulate a vision of what values are worth pursuing and then pursue the opposite. We can decide that a given course of action is rational, moral, and wise—and then proceed to do something else. We can tell ourselves, "I really must think about this" or "I'll think about it tomorrow" (like Scarlett O'Hara) and never do so. We are able to monitor our behavior and ask if it is consistent with our knowledge, convictions, and ideals, and we are also able to evade asking that question. We can choose to focus our mind, and we can choose not to. It is a choice we are constantly obliged to make. No other choice is more fateful for the kind of life we create for ourselves.

The first act of self-responsibility, and the base of all the others, is the act of taking responsibility for being conscious—that is, of bringing an appropriate awareness to our activities.

This issue goes to the heart of our humanity. It is not a matter of culture or of social class. The challenge is universal to our species. On every socioeconomic level we can find people who function relatively consciously and people who function largely unconsciously. Every social or ethnic group includes members who operate mindfully and members who function mindlessly. The knowledge that, as a way of life, awareness is preferable to unawareness, that sight is preferable to blindness, does not require a college education. To possess such knowledge one needs only to be a human being.

Determinism

In the twentieth century we have been assailed with many different versions of the belief that freedom is a delusion and that everyone is determined in all aspects of existence by forces outside any individual's control. The two most influential advocates of this view—which is called *psychological determinism*—were Karl Marx and Sigmund Freud, both of whose philosophies were shaped by a nineteenth-century worldview now totally discredited.

In Marx's version, we are psychological prisoners of our economic class. Our thoughts and actions are determined by the material factors of production and by the way the system of production is organized. Economics is the key to understanding human behavior. Free will does not exist.

In Freud's version, we are psychological prisoners of our instinctual inheritance and our childhood upbringing. Our thoughts and actions are determined by forces operating in the unconscious. We are a battlefield on which blind, primitive impulses intrinsic to our nature clash with internalized parental moral injunctions—while the ego struggles to balance these conflicting claims with the demands of reality. But always, the unconscious has the last word. Free will does not exist.

In Freud's words: "Man is lived by the unconscious. . . . The deeply rooted belief in psychic freedom and choice is quite unscientific and must give ground before the claims of a determinism which governs mental life."

Marx and Freud both reflected the prevailing metaphysics of the nineteenth century. Nineteenth-century thought was deeply influenced by the doctrines of mechanism and materialism, then viewed as the latest word of science. Ultimately, all that existed was matter in motion, and future motion was, theoretically, entirely predictable from past motion, if only one had enough information. All psychology, Freud suggested, one day would be reducible to physiology; and it was the received wisdom of the time that one day all physiology would be reducible to physics. In this scheme, there is no place for free will, choice, or personal responsibility.

This was not a position that Freud or anyone else has ever been able to maintain consistently. Late in life Freud wrote: "[The therapist's task is] to give the patient's ego freedom to chose one way or the other."

What freedom? In a deterministic universe, no freedom exists, neither before nor after psychotherapy. But psychoanalysis required the evasion of this obvious fact. To this day, orthodox analysts twist their brains in the most extraordinary ways to avoid confronting this issue.

Marx and Freud often said things that contradicted their official positions as they would have to, since both wanted to be agents of change. But the fact is that materialism and determinism are the underlying premises of both systems of thought. The metaphysics of mechanism and materialism has long ago been discarded by physics as totally inadequate to describe or understand phenomena of nature. And yet, ironically, its influence in psychology and sociology is still prevalent.

In the United States, B. F. Skinner was the most celebrated psychologist of the twentieth century, and his system of behaviorism is a monument to nineteenth-century materialism. In his *Beyond Freedom and Dignity,* he argues that such notions as free will and self-responsibility are prescientific superstitions. He envisions a world in which people will be "conditioned" to behave as enlightened persons think they should.

There are two things to be said against psychological determinism, whether the doctrine is advanced on economic grounds, as an appeal to instincts, or in reference to some sort of social conditioning. The first is that no empirical evidence supports it: It rests on an act of faith. The second is that no one can maintain a belief in determinism without self-contradiction. I shall briefly state why.

In all its forms the determinist view of mind maintains that whether an individual thinks or not, takes cognizance of the facts of reality or not, places facts above feelings or feelings above facts, everything is determined by forces outside of the individual's control. At any given moment or in any situation, the individual's method of mental functioning is the inevitable product of an endless chain of antecedent factors.

Yet consider this. We are neither omniscient nor infallible. We must work to achieve our knowledge. The mere presence of an idea inside our mind does not prove that the idea is true; many false ideas may enter our consciousness. But if we believe what we *have* to believe, if we are not free to test our ideas against reality and validate or reject them—if the actions and content of our mind, in other words, are determined by factors that may or may not have anything to do with reason, logic, and reality—then we can never know if any conclusion is justified or unjustified, true or false.

Knowledge consists of the correct identification of facts. To know if the contents of our mind *do* constitute knowledge, to know that we have identified the facts correctly, we require a means of testing our conclusions against reality and checking for contradictions. This means is the process of reasoning itself, the noncontradictory integration of all available evidence. It is thus that we validate our conclusions. But this validation is possible only if our capacity to judge is free.

Without this freedom, we cannot maintain logically that any conviction or belief of ours is justified. We can only declare that we feel compelled to believe what we believe. We cannot, without self-contradiction, declare, "A rational examination of the facts supports the doctrine of psychological determinism." We can only declare, "I feel compelled to assert that psychological determinism is true."

Simplified, the argument, declares that: (1) one's political beliefs are determined totally and irresistibly by the political beliefs of one's parents, and (2) I *know* that mine is the only and only true and correct political outlook. If the first statement is true, it becomes logically absurd to assert the second.

Accordingly, if the claim is made that *all* one's beliefs or convictions are determined by factors outside one's control, *no claim to knowledge can be made without logical contradiction.*

A doctrine that annihilates the possibility of knowledge cannot be the appropriate basis of any scientific discussion, or of any other kind of discussion.

Determinism and the Law

Let me make one more observation. Most psychologists and sociologists who advocate determinism also support some version of the insanity defense or the diminished-capacity defense in the courtroom. In essence these defenses consist of asserting that due to a psychiatric condition the accused was powerless to behave other than he or she did. The accused had no choice, couldn't help it, wasn't responsible. But determinism maintains that this is the condition of *everyone*. In the determinist view, no one can help anything he or she does. Why single out the psychotic or the person of alleged diminished capacity? These people suffer the same inability to control behavior that everyone else suffers. These defenses make sense only when contrasted with the normal condition of human beings in which they are free to choose. Note that these defenses do not deny that *normally* we are responsible for our actions. Indeed, they *presuppose* free will as our natural state and assert that the accused is in an abnormal condition.

It is only reasonable to speak of an irresistible impulse if one believes there is such a thing as a resistible impulse. But to a determinist, any impulse that is acted on is proven by that very fact to have been irresistible. To a determinist, action is *never* free. Only hypocrisy allows advocates of this position to resort to some version of the insanity or "couldn't help it" defense when it is expedient to do so.

Am I suggesting the absence of significant differences in the mental state of people considered psychotic or severely disturbed and people considered normal? Not at all; that would be to deny clear evidence. What I am pointing out is that, on the premise of determinism, those differences have nothing to do with the issue of whether one can help one's actions; determinism says that *no one can help anything.**

The Politics of Determinism

The issue of free will versus determinism has many social and political ramifications. According to the premise of free will, people normally are held accountable for their actions; according to the premise of determinism, they are not. At least, that is the way it would work if determinists were logically consistent.

In a determinist framework, however, consistency is impossible and is rarely attempted. Determinism is a doctrine that is often used strategically, in service to particular agendas. Socially and politically, it is less a conviction than a weapon with which to protect those one wishes to protect, leaving the rest entirely answerable for their actions.

In Marxist theory, for example, businessmen are as much helpless prisoners of historical economic forces as are workers; they too are merely acting out a role ordained by the material

---

*For an excellent critique of the "I couldn't help it" excuse in the courtroom, see Alan M. Dershowitz's *The Abuse Excuse.* For a superb overview of our criminal justice system, as it relates to issues of responsibility and nonresponsibility, see *Criminal Justice?*, edited by Robert James Bidinotto; this is the most intelligent discussion of the principle of self-responsibility, as applied to criminals, I have ever read.

factors of production. In reality, however, businessmen are vilified (not to say satanized) by enemies of capitalism, while workers are invariably treated as innocent victims in any clash with management. If a rioting worker destroys machinery, sets fire to a building, or even kills someone, voices are raised to insist that he couldn't help it, due to the pressures of exploitation he endured. Every excuse is made for him. No comparable compassion has ever been shown by Marxist intellectuals to those who own the factors of production. Yet in theory owners and workers are equally innocent pawns of history.

This double standard is by no means confined to those who are influenced by Marxism. So thoroughly have many of Marx's premises permeated the intellectual atmosphere that many people who have never read him nonetheless reflexively react from a Marxist perspective, even today when these ideas have been discarded on the scrap heap of history.

Or if rioters in a poor neighborhood loot stores or beat nearly to death innocent passersby, every excuse is made for their behavior on the grounds that they are the "oppressed" and therefore can't help violating the rights of other people. If, however, a policeman reacts to a lawbreaker with excessive force, *his* "social conditioning" is not upheld as a defense, and the champions of the rioters are in the front lines demanding the policeman be severely punished.

In theory, all of us may be determined by factors beyond our control, but in practice it seems that some of us are more victims of circumstance than others. Non-accountability is a privilege unequally distributed.

If a woman who is physically abused by her husband chooses to remain with him because she fears facing the world on her own until the day when she finally kills him or pays someone else to kill him, her defenders insist that she had no options and did what she had to in the circumstances. If a man is physically abused by his wife (as we now know is a common if unpublicized occurrence), yet chooses to endure her treatment until the day he explodes and kills her or sends her to the hospital, no one suggests that he couldn't help it and had no alternative.

While many women have gone unpunished for killing, or for paying for the killing of, a husband on the grounds that as victims, they were powerless to choose any other course of action, no man has ever successfully used this defense when tried for the murder of his wife, even though he may have been subjected to repeated violence at her hands and felt too psychologically dominated to rebel.

For those who equate "woman" with "victim," women are not accountable for their behavior; only men are accountable. Women are not to be punished for violating another person's rights; only men are to be punished. Women are the helpless prisoners of their social conditioning; men are free agents entirely responsible for what they do. Consequently, men and women are treated very differently by the law for committing the same offenses.*

To qualify for the advantages of psychological determinism, one must establish that one is oppressed. Small wonder that every conceivable group in our society vies with other groups to prove the superiority of their victimhood credentials.

The solution is not to absolve everyone equally on the grounds that no one is responsible for anything. The solution is to reject not only the politicizing of determinism but the doctrine of determinism itself. The solution is the establishment of *a culture of accountability.* Such a culture is one in which we understand that normally we are responsible for our choices and actions and expect to be held accountable by others.

I say "normally" because of course there are circumstances in which we recognize "diminished capacity" or other factors that may limit our full responsibility. But these are exceptions.

---

*For the many forms of legal discrimination against men, see Warren Farrell's shocking book, *The Myth of Male Power.*

To make non-accountability the rule is to poison human relationships and corrupt a society.

In a marriage, an organization, or a culture, only to the extent that people are willing to hold themselves accountable can we have relationships, enterprises, or a world that works. When we deny accountability, we do not carry our own weight: We fail ourselves and we fail others.

Transferring Responsibility from Self to Others

When we chose not to live self-responsibly, we implicitly count on others to make up for our default. We evade accountability in the workplace while counting on the conscientiousness of others to assure that there will still be a company to employ us tomorrow. We shirk holding up our end in a relationship while counting on our partner to care enough to do what is necessary to keep the relationship alive. We refuse to work for a living while counting on the productiveness of others to put food in our mouth, which we obtain by virtue of someone else's generosity, or by the coerced redistribution of wealth via our welfare system, or by crime. We elect to have a baby we cannot afford to raise, without giving five minutes' thought to what being an effective parent requires, speeding into parenthood with all the conscientiousness of a drunk driver, indifferent to the fact that others will be compelled to pay the price of our unconsciousness.

Not long ago, a man named Derek L. consulted me professionally. At the age of thirty-four he was still supported by his mother while he pursued the career of guitar player in a rock band. Derek had rarely earned a day's pay, the exception being an occasional gig, and said he dreaded the idea of having to. When he was arrested for reckless driving, his mother paid his fine. "The thought of having to earn my own living or to be entirely responsible for myself makes me feel so alone in the world," he said earnestly. I asked him how he felt about the burden he was placing on his mother, and he answered, "I feel terrible. But what do you want me to do? Get an ordinary job? Give up my dreams?"

Sometime later in therapy I asked him to do some sentence-completion work. Since sentence-completion exercises figure prominently in my way of doing therapy, and since I give many examples of it throughout this book, let me pause for a word of explanation.

Sentence-completion work as I use it is a tool both of therapy and of research. Having begun working with it in 1970, I have found increasingly more extensive and illuminating ways to utilize it to facilitate self-understanding, melt repressive barriers, liberate self-expression, activate self-healing, and continually test and retest my hypotheses. The essence of the method is that the client is given a sentence stem—an incomplete sentence—and asked to repeat the stem over and over again, each time providing a different ending. Then another follow-up stem is given, and then another, allowing the client to explore a particular area at deeper and deeper levels.*

I gave Derek the stem "If I bring a higher level of consciousness to the choices I make"—and asked him to keep repeating the stem with different endings. His endings included: "I'd feel sick with shame; I'd despise myself; I'd have to go out and get a job like other people do; I'd have to grow up; I'd have to become a man; I'd have to come out of my fantasy life and into reality; I'd have to wake up; I'd have to make it on my own or not make it at all."

On another occasion about two months later, following some rather intensive work, I gave him the stem "As I learn to live more mindfully"—and his endings included: "I'm beginning to like myself; it's hard sometimes; I feel more manly; it's frightening; it's good for my self-respect; I'm learning I do

---

*For more details on the method, see *The Art of Self-Discovery* and *The Six Pillars of Self-Esteem*.

know how to think; I don't feel as disgusted with myself as I used to; I don't know if I can sustain this; it's an uphill battle; I'm scared; I'm discovering things are possible to me I never thought were possible."

That we are free to think or not to think, and to live responsibly or irresponsibly, reflects the essence of what it means to be human. This freedom is our burden, our challenge, our glory.

Self-Reliance and Social Metaphysics

Choosing
to think is our most basic act of self-responsibility. This choice
enables us to grasp and identify reality and to assume the task
of judging what is true or false, reasonable or unreasonable,
right or wrong, good for us or bad for us.

When we reflect on self-responsibility, we ordinarily think of
holding ourselves accountable for our choices and actions in
the world and accepting responsibility for our life and well-
being. But there is a deeper aspect, pertaining to cognition:
our mind's relationship to reality. By this I mean our recognition that only our own understanding can properly guide us
and that we may recognize no authority higher than our mind.
Self-reliance is ultimately reliance on our power to think.

The alternative we encounter at this level is: Do I think for
myself and live off the effort of my own mind? Or do I attempt
to live off the minds of others, bypassing the question of my
own understanding?

Remember that as a species our minds are our basic tool of
survival. Everything that makes us distinctively human—the

food we eat, the clothes we wear, the medicines that heal us, the buildings we inhabit, the airplanes that carry us great distances, the art that inspires us, and the abstract ideas that guide our lives—is a product of the ability to think. No expression of independence or self-reliance is more basic than the exercise of this ability. We cannot take responsibility for our life and well-being if we do not take responsibility for *living mindfully.*

When we choose to avoid intellectual independence, our policy is one of self-abdication. To try to live with minimal thought, authentic understanding, or firsthand judgment is to live secondhand, off the unexamined thoughts, values, and opinions of others. This is the deepest form of *selflessness.* We are reneging on the most basic functions of the self. In this chapter we examine what this means.

Sovereignty

Among children we see the thrust toward sovereignty in such attitudes and behaviors as the following:

A visible delight in the action of his or her mind

A desire for the new, the unexplored, the challenging

A reluctance to accept on faith the platitudes of elders

An insistent use of the word "why?"

Boredom with the routine and indifference to the undemanding

An obsession with questions

A hunger for that which will invoke and stimulate

the full use of his or her powers

Ease and comfort with small acts of independence

As the child grows older, independence expresses itself through the child's formation of his or her own goals. The young person does not look to others to say what should provide enjoyment, how time is to be spent, what to admire, what to pursue, what career to select. He or she needs and wants the help of elders in providing rational guidance and education, but not in providing ready-made goals and values. In the selection of values, the child is a self-generator and welcomes this responsibility. Values proposed by others are scrutinized thoughtfully.

These children do not become pregnant at fourteen "to have a sense of identity" or become criminals "to belong to the gang" or become drug addicts "to feel like somebody." They are not creatures of peer pressure. Rather, they exercise their own judgment and intelligence. They think. They weigh consequences. They project long-range. They practice enlightened selfishness: They ask, "Is this good for me or harmful? Does this serve my life or endanger it?"

This practice of mindfulness results over time in a strong, positive sense of personal identity and self-esteem.

As we grow to adulthood, reality confronts us with increasingly more complex challenges at each succeeding step of our development. The range of thought, knowledge, and decision making required of us at the age of twelve is greater than that required at the age of five; the range required at twenty is greater than at twelve. At each stage, the responsibility required of us involves both cognition and evaluation; we have to acquire knowledge of facts, and we have to pass value judgments and choose goals.

Here are examples, at the high school level, of the kind of issues that might arise:

*"Now that I know how much time school and homework re-
quire of me, and how much time soccer will demand, and how
much time would be needed to participate in the school orchestra,
and how much time I'd like for doing nothing, how do I want to
prioritize my activities? What will I select and what will I forgo?
What matters most to me?"*

*"I am attracted to this girl and want to be with her, but I am
seeing that she has attitudes and values very different from mine.
She doesn't seem to enjoy learning things, and I do. She likes to
get drunk at parties, and I don't admire that. What matters more
to me—her prettiness or the differences in our values? Friends
say she's terrific and I'd be nuts to let her go, but that's not how I
see the situation. Who do I listen to, my friends or my own mis-
givings?"*

*"Our minister says that there is no greater virtue and, for a
woman, no greater glory than self-sacrifice. But he never ex-
plains why I should value other people's wants and needs above
my own. Should I have faith that he's right, as my parents do, or
should I go on pushing for answers that make sense to me?*

At any age, acceptance of responsibility for thinking, choosing, deciding, is not automatic. The decision to function as an
independent, self-responsible entity is not wired into the brain
by nature. It is a challenge to which each one of us responds
positively or negatively *by choice.*

By the time we are adults we have been bombarded with
countless value judgments by parents, teachers, and peers, to say
nothing of the culture at large. Our parents have conveyed, explicitly or implicitly, verbally or nonverbally, messages concerning how we are to view men, women, our bodies, our sexuality,
love, marriage, people of different religious, philosophical, or
political orientations, and the world in general. We have been
exposed to any number of ideas about work, ambition, money,

and success. We receive messages about what constitutes the "good life." To what extent do we think about these views and to what extent do we absorb them without thinking? To what extent will *we* decide and to what extent do we allow others to decide for us?

From the perspective of culture, we live in a sea of philosophical messages. Every society contains a network of values, beliefs, and assumptions, not all of which are named explicitly but which nonetheless are part of the human environment—the "sea" in which we swim. Ideas that are not identified overtly but are conveyed tacitly can be harder to call into question, even for a fairly independent mind, precisely because they are absorbed by a process that largely bypasses the conscious intelligence. We possess what might be called a "cultural unconscious," a set of implicit beliefs about nature, reality, human beings, man-woman relationships, good and evil, that reflects the knowledge, understanding, and values of a historical time and place. To be sure, there are many differences among people within a given culture in their beliefs at this level. There are serious differences in how consciously these beliefs are held and to what extent any individual may challenge them. But at least some of these beliefs reside in every psyche in a given society, and without ever being the subject of explicit awareness.

The measure of our intellectual independence (and maturity) is *what it occurs to us to question.* No one has time or motivation to question everything. Many issues do not matter to us that much. Our independence and capacity for critical thought are most needed when the issues affect us directly in the daily conduct of life.

A layperson, for example, having no particular interest in physics, would have neither the competence nor the interest to challenge some piece of "received wisdom" in that field. Neither would he or she hold any strong convictions on the subject, one way or the other. Independence and rationality in this instance are knowing that all we have is hearsay, not firsthand knowledge. While a pretentious, nonauthentic person might make pronouncements at cocktail parties about "the newest findings in physics" without actually knowing what the words meant or what evidence supported them, an independent man or woman would not. A key expression of independence is taking responsibility for knowing what we are talking about.

An independent person listens critically and thoughtfully to the advice given, say, by a physician or lawyer, and often chooses to follow it without firsthand knowledge of its rightness. This is called taking a calculated risk. The important word here is *calculated*. This is why, when the stakes are high enough, we often solicit a second opinion. We know that we do not know and want to be as intelligent about our risk taking as we can be.

But when it comes to such questions as "For what purpose should I live? How should I deal with other people? What deserves my admiration and what does not? By what principles should I act? What kind of life should I strive to create for myself?" *An independent person knows that there are no "experts" to whom one can safely surrender one's intellect.*

It hardly needs to be said that we learn from each other and influence each other. Nor is it denied that we exist in a historical context no one can entirely escape. We do not think in a vacuum. Just the same—and this is the important point—there is a profound distinction between those whose fundamental orientation is to think for themselves and those whose notion of thinking is to recycle uncritically the opinions of other people.

This is what is wrong with justifying one's viewpoint by appeals to "tradition." Tradition (meaning the choices and beliefs of those who have come before us) may be right or wrong in any given case. If we decide, as an independent act of thought and judgment, that certain traditional principles are grounded in reason and reality, that is one thing. To follow them only because our ancestors did, is quite another.

Intellectual sovereignty, self-reliance, and self-responsibility are rooted in a firm *sense of reality*. This means a deep respect for facts. What is, *is*. Things are what they are. Truth is not obliterated by the refusal to see it. Facts are not annihilated by the pretense that they do not exist. If a man is an alcoholic, he is an alcoholic, even if the whole family refuses to acknowledge it. If a scientist fakes her research, she is a fraud, even if her dishonesty remains undetected. If a priest molests children, no profession of piety alters the nature of his act. If my teenager has become addicted to drugs, that is his condition, whether or not he or I acknowledge it. If a new discovery contradicts and disconfirms my assumptions, that is a *fact*, whether or not I choose to think about it. What is, *is*, and a person's deep inner connection to this truth is what I mean by a sense of reality.

To be genuine, intellectual independence must be anchored in the real. The "independence" of a psychotic is not what I am describing. To the extent that we exist in delusion, we depend for our survival and well-being on those who are better related to reality than we are. *Realism* is essential to self-responsibility.

I want to pause on this point because it must be fully understood as context for the discussion of psychological dependence, or "social metaphysics," that follows.

To become fully competent to master the challenges of life, and thus attain independence, we must grasp and respect the distinction between the real and the unreal, between facts, on the one hand, and wishes, hopes, fears, and fantasies on the other. To be an accomplished artist, scientist, businessperson, or writer and to dream of being one are not the same thing. To be a person of accomplishment and merely to be *believed* to be one by other people, are not the same thing either. A delusion in someone else's consciousness is no better than a delusion in one's own.

Barriers to Sovereignty

Any number of factors can obstruct evolution to intellectual autonomy and self-responsibility.

A child may experience an assault on his or her self-esteem in the early years of life by destructive parenting. Individuation may be arrested, and the first stages of intellectual self-trust and self-confidence never attained. Why struggle to think if we have no belief in the efficacy of our minds? Or if we are persuaded that human existence is such a nightmare of irrationality that thinking is useless?

There are children who are starved for the smallest experience of visibility or esteem from their parents. To win recognition and acceptance becomes the ruling passion of their life, which later they will transfer to other people. To feel that they belong *with* people, they are willing to belong *to* them. They give up anything for "love."

Some dominating parents are so eager to control the thinking and feeling of a child that they begin pounding in their messages at a very early age. In effect, they take up residence in the child's psyche. This can occur to such an extent that the child is lost inside the parents' perspective from the very beginning and gains almost no independent sense of reality. In my experience, even a very intelligent child is susceptible to this imprisonment when the parents are perceived as brilliant, charismatic, and devastatingly self-assured. The parents' eagerness to implant what is "true" and "right" becomes a barrier to the child's firsthand understanding. Even when the parents' ideas are valid, they are not properly "owned" by the child, and so the child's cognitive relationship to the world remains secondhand.

Some parents implicitly or explicitly convey that "What you think and feel is unimportant. What is important is what others think and feel." Some children internalize this belief, thereby sabotaging their own development.

Some parents seem to ask, "Who are you to hold your own opinions or imagine your views count for anything?" Some children surrender and agree.

But apart from the issue of destructive childhood experiences, temptations to give up the quest for autonomy or sovereignty are intrinsic to the human condition.

First of all, thinking requires an effort. Thinking is mental *work*. Operating at an appropriate level of consciousness in different situations and contexts does not happen instinctively or automatically. To generate the energy required is an act of choice. We must act against the gravitational pull of inertia. A simpler way to express this is to say that we must overcome any impulse to laziness. "Laziness" is not a concept psychologists ordinarily talk about, and yet some aspects of human behavior cannot be understood without it. We are all intimately aware of the simple disinclination to exert effort. It is the most primitive challenge that thinking and sovereignty must confront and conquer.

Next, a policy of mindfulness—a policy of thinking practiced as a way of life—stands in the way of indulging desires or emotions that clash with our understanding and convictions. If we remain fully conscious, the contradictions stare us in the face, inhibiting our impulsiveness, like a stop sign before a rush of irrationality. As one therapy client remarked self-mockingly, "When you want to do something stupid, consciousness can be such a killjoy."

Then there is the simple fact that our mind is fallible. We can make an error at any step of the thinking process. If we act on our error, we may suffer pain or defeat or destruction. And it will be our responsibility, our "fault." If we act on our own judgment and turn out to be mistaken, we cannot reasonably pass the buck to anyone else. Whereas—and this is the great temptation for some people—if we forego independence and let others decide, the error or disaster is not our responsibility and we are not to blame. If we dread accountability, we dread and avoid independent thinking (and vice versa). The willingness to confront this issue and overcome it can be a heroic project.

A policy of independent thinking may bring us into conflict with the opinions and judgments of others. Sometimes these others are very important to us. If we dread their animosity or disapproval, we may seek to avoid it by not thinking for ourselves. (For the first time in our life, we begin to think about politics and suspect that our spouse's passionately held views are mistaken. *What will we do?*) If we don't take independent stands, we need not challenge or provoke anyone. Young girls are often told, "Never do anything that will upset anyone." This is an injunction to avoid independent thinking and to conform to the unexamined beliefs of others. Young boys also receive such messages, if not always so directly. Yet, with or without these messages, many people choose to value harmony with others above the judgment of their own mind. They value belonging above self-esteem.

The problem is not that we want to be liked. Who does not prefer being liked to being disliked? The problem is where this desire stands in the hierarchy of our values. Does it stand at the peak, above everything else, above integrity and self-respect? The question is not whether we want to be liked, but what are we willing to give in exchange? Are we willing to give our mind and our self-esteem? To surrender our sovereignty? The tragedy for many people is that the answer is *yes.* I say "tragedy" because so much suffering is traceable to this surrender.

Of course, no one can renounce independent thinking altogether. What we are examining here is invariably a matter of degree. There are people who exhibit a high degree of independent thinking, and there are people who exhibit close to none. It is a continuum.

The decision to forgo independence is not made in a moment, nor is it a matter of a single choice. It is the product of a long succession of choices in a long succession of events. In one instance, the motive may be a disinclination to exert effort; in another, fear of making a mistake; in yet another, dread of being in conflict with significant others.

The more we retreat from the responsibility of independence, the more daunting the prospect of such responsibility appears. We feel more and more unequal to the challenge. How can we rely on a mind we have learned not to trust?

Or again, the more we surrender to the fear of disapproval, the more we lose face in our eyes, the more desperate we become for *someone's* approval. Within us there is a void that should have been occupied by self-esteem. When we attempt to fill it with the approval of others instead, the void grows deeper and the hunger for acceptance and approval grows stronger.

This leads me to the problem I call "social metaphysics," discussed next.

Social Metaphysics

Fear of intellectual independence is the deepest form of fearing self-responsibility. It can exist in varying degrees of severity. What are its consequences when it is the dominant element in a person's psychology?

When we fail to grow into proper independence, default on the need to think, and never transfer the source of our approval from the environment to the self, a void is created within us. The need for knowledge remains, as does the need for values and for a sense of worth. Inevitably, we turn to others to fill these needs because the vacuum is unbearable. We feel, wordlessly, that *we* do not know, but others seem to know; somehow they possess control of that mysterious unknowable, reality. We feel that we do not love or respect ourselves, but if others are favorably impressed by us, then we can be a worthy person. They hold our self-esteem in their hands.

This obsession with the approval of others should not be confused with the perfectly normal desire to be seen, understood, and appreciated for our *real* character traits and accomplishments. We all want to be psychologically visible, as I have discussed in previous books. We want to feel linked to other human beings through, in part, an exchange of visibility. This happens when we are mirrors to one another, giving and receiving appropriate verbal and nonverbal feedback. But there is a difference between wishing others to *perceive* our value and wishing them to *create* it through their approval. It is this latter state we are examining.

Through slow, imperceptible stages, beginning with the earliest years of life, the concept of "reality" that forms in the consciousness I am describing is *the-world-as-perceived-by-others*. One exists not in a universe of facts but in a *universe of people*. People (their views, beliefs, feelings), not facts, are "reality." People, not our own minds, are our basic means of survival. So, to survive and assure our well-being, it is *others* who must be understood, pleased, placated, deceived, maneuvered, manipulated, or obeyed (depending on other personality variables). It is success at this task that becomes the gauge of efficacy at living and, therefore, the standard of self-esteem.

Objective reality has very little significance to such a consciousness. What counts is not what *is* but what people (significant others) *believe* is. Therefore, to grasp and successfully satisfy the expectations, conditions, demands, terms, and values of others is experienced as the deepest, most urgent need. The reward is a temporary diminution of anxiety, the feeling that one is, after all, appropriate to life and to what life requires . . . *as determined by others*.

This is "social metaphysics."

Remember that in philosophy "metaphysics" is one's view of the ultimate nature of reality. To the person I am describing, reality is *other people*. In his or her mind, in the automatic connections of his or her consciousness, people occupy the place which, in the mind of an autonomous, self-responsible individual, is occupied by reality.

Social metaphysics is the psychological condition of one who holds the minds and perspectives of other people, not objective reality, as the ultimate authority and frame of reference.

In its purest form, social metaphysics can be understood as follows:

Ultimately, things are as you say they are. I am as you desire me. I am as good—or bad—as you declare me to be.

The basic dependence here is cognitive—I could even say *spiritual*—a policy of functioning within a belief system established by others, of living by the guidance of values prescribed by others, absorbed without any independent process of reasoning, and for which one does not take intellectual responsibility.

What this produces, at best, when the social metaphysician is successful, is not self-esteem but *pseudo* self-esteem. Having no genuine ground within the individual, it is intrinsically unreliable. Anxiety is always waiting in the wings.

Since this pseudo self-esteem rests on the ability to deal with the-world-as-perceived-by-others, the fear of disapproval or condemnation is the fear of being pronounced unfit for reality, inadequate to the challenges of life, devoid of personal worth—a verdict the social metaphysician feels whenever he or she is rejected. One client said to me, agony in his eyes, "If I am not responded to favorably, I feel as if I am exiled from existence. Not just my sense of worth but my being itself feels undercut."

A businessman I once knew, a multimillionaire, was obsessively concerned with what everyone thought of him, even the office boy. He felt driven to win the boy's approval or liking. He would make himself charming to win a favorable response. Clearly he had nothing practical to gain from the boy. It was the not boy as an actual person that he sought to charm but the boy as a symbol of other people, all other people, mankind at large. The thought behind his behavior was not "The office boy is a potential provider who will take care of me and guide me" but "I am acceptable to other people. People who are not me approve of me, they regard me as a good human being. Therefore I am worthy of living."

Many years ago I knew a professor of philosophy who had given a great deal of thought and study to the subject of religion and decided there was no rational basis for a belief in God. He saw the notion of a supernatural being as irrational and often destructive in its effects on believers. Yet he avoided the issue of atheism versus theism in his writings and lectures, refused to commit himself on the subject publicly, and every Sunday attended church with his parents and relatives. He would not tell himself that his motive was fear, that he was terrified to stand against his family, that violent arguments of any kind made him panicky, and that he desperately wanted to be accepted by everyone. Instead he told himself that he could not bear to hurt his elderly parents, who were devoutly religious and who would be dismayed by his lack of faith. In many respects I was fond of this man; I admired his intellect and found him very decent in his dealings with people. I wondered aloud to him how he could take his own convictions with so little seriousness. "And besides," he answered, "announcing my atheism might hurt me professionally," ignoring the fact that any number of professors were known atheists and it mattered to almost no one.

I asked, "How can you not be willing to take more responsibility for your ideas and stand behind them?"

"Well, that's just who I am," was his unhappy reply.

A successful novelist and playwright once came to a lecture of mine, and afterwards came back to my apartment with a few other people for coffee and conversation. He had become famous while still in his twenties for a marvelous thriller I had much enjoyed. We began talking about fame, and he remarked, "It's funny. When you become successful the cliché is that you then snub the people who were once your friends. But for me, and I suspect for many others, the exact opposite happens. Your old friends snub you. They don't know what to do with you. And they're envious. *They* change in their behavior toward you but complain that it's *you* who've changed." When he said this, he looked deeply hurt.

"That would make an interesting play," someone offered. "An interesting reversal of the conventional idea."

At first the playwright grew excited at the suggestion and began thinking aloud, projecting a serious drama. "This is one of the most painful issues in my life," he remarked. "And it's important in what it says about many people's psychology." Then he stopped abruptly. His enthusiasm vanished as his whole manner changed in some way I could not decipher, and he said, "No. I think I'll do it as a comedy. Not be so heavy about it."

I was perplexed. "You could, I suppose," I answered. "But why? What changed your mind?"

He replied awkwardly and a bit defensively, "The serious version might antagonize people." I thought, He still wants to be loved by the very people who rejected him. In some way he feels he needs them for his survival. I recall feeling a wave of quiet sadness at this realization. This was more than thirty years ago and I was not surprised that he never wrote the play at all, neither as a drama nor as a comedy.

The behavior and state of mind that I first named "social metaphysics" in the mid-1950s, attracted my attention and challenged my understanding some years earlier, long before I entered clinical practice. I recall, for instance, a boy called Lloyd who lived across the street from me when I was thirteen. Lloyd confided one day that his uncle, who was a traveling salesman, would bring back labels from expensive New York shops and Lloyd would have his mother sew these labels on his clothes to impress his friends.

"But," I protested, mystified, "you know that none of this is *real*. You know that your mother buys your clothes from much less expensive stores right here in Toronto. And anyway, *who cares* where your clothes come from?"

Lloyd smiled at my bewilderment, a smile of older, superior wisdom, and answered, "People will *think* the clothes come from New York."

Across a space of fifty years I recall my consternation at his response and my struggle to grasp the nature of a consciousness that worked as Lloyd's worked, with his values and outlook on life.

I saw a connection I could not then identify between Lloyd's mental processes and those of my own mother, who was eternally preoccupied with "what people will think." To my mother, impressions seemed to count for everything and reality for nothing. This became the focus of many conflicts between us when she urged me to say things and behave in ways that I thought phony and ridiculous and she thought "made a good impression." (I was amused to read, decades later, that behaviorist B. F. Skinner was troubled by the same trait in *his* mother. Was his solution to produce a school of psychology that denied the reality or significance of thinking so it didn't *matter* what people thought?)

In adolescence I became increasingly aware of many people's preoccupations with appearances and with being liked, at the expense of truth, facts, or logic. I saw that a delusion created in someone else's mind could rank very high with them, while reality could easily be dismissed as irrelevant. I thought that this was something very important about people, and I spent many hours trying to understand.

Understanding came in my twenties, when I began to practice psychotherapy. Two cases were decisive. The first was an aspiring artist, a young woman my own age, whose every statement, voice tone, and gesture seemed calculated for the effect she imagined it would have on other people. She suffered a humiliating hunger to be thought intelligent and artistically talented by whomever she met. The second was a young student of philosophy who complained that as soon as he began to study some philosopher's system, he somehow got lost inside it, felt utterly trapped by its perspective, so that his own convictions became remote and almost meaningless to him— as if his mind had been taken over by the person he was studying. He, too, complained of a burning, inexhaustible need for approval and of great difficulty in holding onto thoughts unshared by others. My efforts to understand their inner processes led to the first identification of the problem I am describing in this chapter—a consciousness that has replaced reality with the-world-as-perceived-by-others. In later years I learned a great deal about different types of social metaphysicians and about different patterns of motivation.

Some are social metaphysicians who are so deeply imprisoned by their orientation that no alternative occurs to them. While it is impossible to be completely devoid of autonomy, it is so minor an element in their psychology that their dependence and avoidance of self-responsibility feel utterly normal and natural. The-world-as-perceived-by-others is all there is. For some social metaphysicians, the only notion of rebellion or independence is to defy whatever significant others believe and mindlessly assert the opposite. Teenagers, for instance, may be compulsively drawn to whatever would most outrage their parents and imagine that that is autonomy. They have no more concern for reason or objectivity than the most abject conformist. In both cases, others dictate the terms of their existence.

Other social metaphysicians suffer an acute awareness of their state, reproach themselves for it, and feel powerless to change. Yet the restless longing for a better mode of being persists.

Social metaphysicians can differ in many ways, as I indicate below, but certain key traits are constant:

- They lack their own firm, unyielding concept of existence, facts, reality, as apart from the judgments, beliefs, opinions, feelings of others.

- They experience a fundamental sense of helplessness and powerlessness, deeper than any surface confidence in particular areas.

- They have a profound fear of other people and an implicit belief that other people control that mysterious realm, reality.

- Their self-esteem—or, more precisely, their pseudo self-esteem—depends on the responses of significant others.

The most fundamental of these traits, and this cannot be overemphasized, is *the absence of a firm, independent sense of objective reality.*

We see this, for example, in the teenager who has a baby "so someone will love me," with no thought as to who will pay for it or what will be the consequences for her life or the life she has brought into existence.

We see it in the politician whose sole measure of greatness is the number of people he can persuade to believe his lies.

We see it in the employee who appropriates the accomplishments of a coworker and hypnotizes him- or herself into enjoying (and believing) the praise offered by the boss.

We see it in the rioter who burns down a neighborhood, "in protest against the system," with no thought to how he will obtain his daily necessities now that there are no stores to serve him and no businesses that will move back into the area.

We see it in intellectuals who operate as apologists for dictatorships ("you can't make an omelet without breaking eggs") and who, when the magnitude of the atrocities can no longer be evaded, proclaim themselves to have been "misguided idealists" who bear no moral responsibility for the horrors they spend decades denying or condoning. (Talk about lack of accountability—this may be the ultimate example of its immorality in the twentieth century.)

When we first grasp the idea of social metaphysics, we are likely to think of its most obvious form, the conventional conformist. This is the person who accepts the world and its prevailing values ready-made; reason and judgment play little if any role in the process. What is true? What others say is true. What is right? What others believe is right. How should we live? As others live. Why do we work for a living? Because we are *supposed* to. Why do we get married? Because we are *supposed* to. Why do we have children? Because one is *supposed* to. Why does one go to church? Oh, please don't start discussing religion, you might upset someone. This is lack of self-responsibility at the most blatant level.

If a person such as I am describing is raised in a world that values science, he or she may become a scientist and may even, within limits, think independently about some issues and sometimes challenge the views of colleagues, *as expected*. Or such a person may become a hard worker in a business organization, *as expected*. Or become a devoted wife and mother, *as expected*. He or she may attempt to lead a useful, productive life, *as expected*. Within parameters laid down by others, he or she may exhibit some measure of individuality—without ever thinking deeply about those parameters.

In a society in which racism is acceptable and regarded as normal and appropriate, a social metaphysician may embrace it eagerly. Pseudo self-esteem is then nurtured by *not* belonging to a particular racial or ethnic group and being superior to it. In a society in which racism is out of fashion and condemned, a social metaphysician may sing songs to the effect that we are all brothers and sisters. Pseudo self-esteem is then nurtured by the idea of being politically correct and also by the idea that if we are all equal, all one, there is no need to feel inferior.

Earlier in this century, a young social metaphysician of modest gifts might have graduated high school and gone on to a lifetime of conscientious if unspectacular work in the family hardware store. Today, in a world of disappearing fathers; leaders without credibility; cynicism about values; contempt for work; popular music that celebrates violence, torture, and death; and drug dealers as role models, such a person may join a neighborhood gang to gain some sense of belonging and shoot some passerby (or shoot up heroin) as the price of acceptance by the only "family" available. When asked why he participated in a drive-by shooting, a sixteen-year-old boy said, "I wanted my friends to respect me."

Within this category of social metaphysicians, there are immense differences in intelligence, honesty, ambition, and ability. In a culture such as ours, one that holds a diversity of values and models and a diversity of subcultures, significant differences in discrimination and judgment are exercised in their choice of authorities. They may change their allegiance more than once during a lifetime. What remains constant is the hunger to belong at the expense of their own sovereignty. Despairing of winning their parents' love, for example, they may elect to belong to a guru and seek "love" in an ashram in exchange for the renunciation of their intellect.

While the conventional social metaphysician may occasionally enjoy dominating and controlling another human being, that is not central to his or her motivation, just as rage and hatred are not central (although they may certainly be part of the story). But they *are* central to another type of social metaphysician whose being is organized around the quest for power.

Power-seeking social metaphysicians range from the petty tyrants of everyday life who make employees or family members miserable, to dictators who destroy whole countries. We often find that their childhood is marked by severe violence, brutality, and humiliation. Among the most extreme examples are Adolf Hitler and Saddam Hussein, both of whom were beaten mercilessly as children. The obsession with destructive power often seems to have its roots in early experiences of traumatic powerlessness. Not that these experiences *determine* what these persons grow into. People who have such experiences may be wounded by them but in most cases do not turn into monsters. They learn better survival skills than that, or they do not make these experiences the most important fact of their existence. In contrast, the power-seeking type creates a life path from this tragic beginning. And even this beginning is not invariable: Hermann Göring, the Nazi leader, for example, was a pampered child.

To this type, the conventional social metaphysician's route to pseudo self-esteem is too frighteningly precarious; the specter of possible failure and defeat looms too large to be endured. The power seeker feels too unsure of his or her ability to gain love and approval because the sense of inferiority is too overwhelming. And the humiliation of dependence is infuriating. The conventional type is willing to endure the uncertainty of "free-market" social metaphysical competition in which other people's esteem must be won *voluntarily*. By contrast, the power seeker deceives, manipulates, and coerces the minds of others to be able to *command* respect, obedience, and love.

King Frederick William of Prussia would have his subjects beaten, while shouting at them: "You must not fear me, you must love me!"

In our century, think of a brute standing on the balcony of his palace, the blood of millions dripping from his fingers, beaming down at a ragged mob gathered there to honor him—the brute knowing that the scene is a fraud of his own staging, courtesy of his soldier's bayonets—while his chest swells in satisfaction as he basks in the warmth of his victim's "adoration." This is what is meant by the absence of a sense of reality.

The rage and hatred that such people feel toward other human beings extends ultimately to existence, to a universe that does not allow them to have their irrationality and their self-esteem too, a universe that links irrationality to pain, guilt, and terror. To defeat the reality they have never chosen to respect, to defy reason and logic, and to get away with it becomes a burning lust to experience the one sort of "efficacy" they can project. And since, for social metaphysicians, reality means other people, the goal of their existence is to impose their will on others, to compel others to provide them with a universe in which the irrational works. Fidel Castro's last-ditch stand to make communism succeed in Cuba, after its unworkability has been demonstrated on a world scale at the cost of incalculable human suffering, is illustrative of this pattern of rebellion against reason.

Of course there are tamer versions of the power-seeking mentality a little closer to home than Cuba.

As I have already conveyed, this power need not be political. There are parents who seek relief from feelings of impotence by overcontrolling and sometimes terrorizing their children. There are presidents of corporations who promote not according to ability but to the capacity for obsequiousness (although the market tends to penalize this policy). There are rich relatives who delight in torturing potential heirs with their capricious demands to underscore their dominion over them. There are professors who enjoy undercutting the intellectual self-confidence of students by tossing off incomprehensible contradictions as knowledge and sneering at anyone who challenges them. And there are, no doubt, nasty little Girl Scout and Boy Scout leaders who get sadistic pleasure from browbeating children.

Faced with the question, What am I to do with my life? or What will make me happy? the ordinary social metaphysician seeks the answers among the standards and values of a particular culture or subculture: respectability, financial success, marriage, family, professional competence, prestige, and the like.

In a decent society, some of the values selected may have much to recommend them. In contrast, faced with the question, How am I to make my existence endurable? the power seeker seeks the answer in aggressive and destructive action aimed at the external object of fear: other people. The destructive action need not by physical; not all power seekers have a stomach for violence. The assault may be intellectual, even spiritual. *Whatever the form, the desire to control and manipulate other people is the desire to defeat reality and make one's wishes omnipotent.*

Yet another type is what I call the "spiritual" social metaphysician. This type may not seek to please and placate people, or to gain power over them, although sometimes they do. Often this type conveys that he or she is a little too good for this world. Love and esteem must be given him or her not for any quality of character or for anything actually done—*doing* is so vulgar—but for an alleged quality of being. And what is this quality? Nothing that can be communicated.

In other words, the claim to self-esteem here is based on the possession of a superior kind of soul, a soul that is not mind, not thoughts, not values, not anything specifiable, but an ineffable composite of indefinable longings, incommunicable insights, and impenetrable mystery. Sometimes this type likes to give the audience a clue, announcing grandly, "Who I am, in my essence, is love!" A client in therapy once told me this, offering it in justification for, at the age of thirty-eight, still being supported by her father.

"I love *everybody,*" declared a "new ager" at a conference I attended. And, in a joking manner that deceived no one, added, *"And everybody had bloody well better love me!"*

As this orientation becomes increasingly familiar and socially acceptable, it ceases to characterize a unique type and disappears into the category of conventional social metaphysician within the context of its own particular subculture.

◆ ◆ ◆

Then there is the "independent" social metaphysician. I characterize this type as a counterfeit individualist. This is the person who rebels against the status quo for the sake of being rebellious, whose pseudo self-esteem is tied to the idea of being a nonconformist.

This is the rebel whose notion of independence is to assert "everything stinks." This is the "individualist" who proves it by scorning money, marriage, jobs, baths, haircuts—*and any kind of accountability.*

Confronted by the feeling of inadequacy to conventional standards and expectations, the counterfeit individualist produces a solution, announcing, "whatever is, *is wrong.*" Confronted with the problem of feeling like an outcast, he or she declares that being an outcast is proof of superiority.

This thinking ignores the two opposing reasons why we may be outside of society: Because our standards are higher than those of society, or because they are lower. Because we are above society or below it. Because we are too good or not good enough.

With the failure to develop a sense of objective reality that characterizes the other types of social metaphysicians, the "independent" social metaphysician sees existence as a clash between his or her whims and the whims of other people. The only question is whose will prevail? Reason, objectivity, and reality are not part of the equation.

At a party a well-known sixties radical once said to me, "There is no reality. There's only my way of defining reality and someone else's way. If my way prevails, if other people sign on for it, that's 'reality.' If I say blue is red, and others agree, then blue *is* red. If I say a piece of crap is great art, and I can persuade you and enough other people to agree, then it *is* great art. Don't you get it? Looting isn't looting, and murder isn't murder if enough people agree to call it something else. That's what the struggle for power is ultimately all about—who gets to say what things are."

While there may be posturing as a dedicated crusader, with sworn devotion to some idea or goal, the primary motivation is negative rather than positive: to be *against* rather than *for*. This counterfeit individualist does not originate or struggle for values that are personally meaningful but merely rebels against the standards of others, as if the absence of conformity, rather than the presence of independent, rational judgment, were the hallmark of self-reliance and true sovereignty. This nihilistic mentality is magnificently portrayed in Dostoyevsky's *The Possessed*.

The "independent" social metaphysician is the brother- or sister-in-spirit of the power seeker, and often only historical circumstance determines which path a given individual takes. In the political arena, for instance, Nazism and communism attracted many "independent" social metaphysicians who made an effortless transition to the psychology of power seeking. They found a form of togetherness for which they were eagerly willing to renounce their "independence."

In a culture where rationality, productiveness, respect for individual rights, and simple sanity are prevailing values, if only on a commonsense level, social metaphysicians of the "independent" type tend to remain on the fringes of society. But in a culture such as ours, the pressure resulting from an intellectual vacuum can fling them up from their cellars to the pinnacles of prestige in an extended Fool's Day orgy. Then we see the spread of eccentric mediocrity, we see the glorification of unconsciousness, we see philosophical and artistic psychosis elevated to grandeur. One sees whims for the sake of whims, absurdity for the sake of absurdity, destruction for the sake of destruction, becoming *fashionable*. Welcome to the modern world.

Finally, there is a type of social metaphysician who differs in important respects from the foregoing varieties. I call this type the "ambivalent" social metaphysician.

This is the man or woman who, notwithstanding a major surrender to the authority of others,, has still preserved a significant degree of intellectual sovereignty. The ambivalent type retains far more authentic independence than the other types. The self-abdication tends to be limited to the area where all social metaphysicians are most vulnerable—the realm of values.

Men and women of the ambivalent type may not question the basic values of their social environment but are often indifferent to them, paying them only perfunctory respect. Without originating values of their own, they often withdraw, surrendering those aspects of reality to others. They tend to restrict their activity and concern chiefly to the sphere of work, where their self-reliance and sovereignty are greatest.

Their social metaphysics is revealed in their humiliating hunger for approval and acceptance and in what they are willing to surrender to win it. Their superiority to other types of social metaphysicians is revealed, not only in their greater independence, but also by their desire to *earn*, through real achievements, the esteem they long for. They find it hard to find pleasure in admiration not based on standards they can respect. Often they are tortured and disgusted with their own dependency. Among this type are men and women of distinguished accomplishments and creative originality, whose tragedy lies in the contrast between their social lives and their lives as achievers.

I recall a brilliant neurophysiologist I knew some years ago, Robert L., who carried within him precisely the ambivalence I am describing. An independent, innovative, and highly critical thinker in the field of his scientific interests, he was boringly conventional in his personal life. He craved people's good opinion and despised himself for it and for the things he was willing to say and do to make a favorable impression. He was reluctant to express any value judgment for which he could not know in advance the position of his listeners. He could speak freely about matters of science because he perceived these as neutral in value. "It's not that I don't have values," he once said to me sadly. "But my soul lives underground. It's humiliating to be this afraid of people. I know that I'm afraid to live. That's my terrible secret. And tomorrow, at the lab, I'll tell myself this conversation never happened."

None of these types belongs to mutually exclusive categories. Any given social metaphysician may exhibit traits of several types. I have merely isolated certain *dominant trends* that make different patterns of motivation intelligible. In my experience, the concept of social metaphysics makes many aspects of human behavior less mysterious.

Obedience to Authority

The twentieth century has been marked by a spectacle of human beings murdering other human beings in unimaginable numbers, from Nazi Germany to Soviet Russia and Red China to Cambodia. To interpret this fact as evidence of humanity's innate cruelty is to miss the point. Especially if we remember the kind of brainwashing that was often necessary to turn ordinary people into killers.

Viewed globally, the overwhelming majority of these killings were not for personal gain, and they do not fall into the category of individual crime. They were not "selfish" acts. Most of the people who did the killing were obeying authority, following orders, fighting for a cause, submerging self and personal judgment in the service of something allegedly greater than themselves that was more important than their private egos or individual consciences.

To quote Arthur Koestler in *Janus:*

> Throughout human history, the ravages caused by excesses of individual self-assertion are quantitatively negligible compared to the numbers slain *ad majorem*

gloriam out of a self-transcending devotion to a flag, a leader, a religious faith or political conviction. Man has always been prepared not only to kill but also to die for good, bad, or completely hare-brained causes. What can be a more valid proof for the reality of the urge toward self-transcendence?

When we are acting in the name of "something greater than ourselves," we lose the sense of personal responsibility for our actions and become capable of evils we would not commit on our own behalf. The surrender of self releases us from accountability. "For the good of mankind, people have to be sacrificed." "I was only obeying my superiors."

To experience another human being in his or her humanity, we need to be in touch with our own. To feel responsible for our actions, we need to experience ourselves, not some external authority, as the source of them. This is why every dictator knows that the individual ego is his enemy and seeks to destroy it by demanding its surrender to something "greater." No one inveighed more passionately against "selfishness" than Hitler. "In the hunt for their own happiness," he warned, "people fall all the more out of heaven into hell."

It is useful, in this context, to recall the famous Stanley Milgrim experiment, reported in his book *Obedience to Authority.* Milgrim and his associates arranged that a group of experimental subjects, drawn from the general population, would be led to believe that they were serving the goals of science by administering increasingly severe and painful electric shocks to volunteer subjects who failed to answer certain questions correctly. The purpose of the experiment, they were told, was to study the effects of punishment on learning. Unaware that this latter group of subjects were playacting, that the screams and cries to be released were only a performance and the electric shocks were not real, the aggressor subjects were being tested, unbeknownst to themselves, on their willingness to surrender moral autonomy to the voice of authority. Numerous controls were built into the experiment to rule out any element of personal aggressiveness. The presiding experimenter had no power over the volunteer subjects and no financial rewards to offer for compliance. He could only say things like, "Please continue." Or, "The experiment requires that you continue." Every factor was eliminated except one: the disposition to obey perceived authority.

In advance of conducting the experiment, Milgrim invited a group of psychiatrists to predict the outcome. "With remarkable similarity they predicted that virtually all the subjects would refuse to obey the experimenter," he reports. The thirty-nine psychiatrists who answered Milgrim's questionnaire shared the view that "most people would not go beyond the one hundred fifty volts (when the victims asked the first time to be released). They expected that only 4 percent would reach three hundred volts and that only a pathological fringe of one in a thousand would administer the highest shock on the board.

Under the instructions of the presiding scientist/authority figure, ignoring the cries and screams of the "victims," more than 60 percent of the Yale subjects kept pressing the dummy buttons up to the limit of four hundred fifty volts, even though this voltage was clearly marked "Danger—severe shock."

This experiment has been repeated in a number of universities throughout the world, with essentially the same results. In other countries, the percentage of people who obeyed to the upper limit of voltage was generally higher than at Yale. In Munich, it was 85 percent.

Milgrim writes:

> For a man to feel responsible for his actions, he must sense that the behavior has flowed from "the self." In the situation we have studied, subjects have precisely the opposite view of their actions—namely, they see

them as originating in the motives of the other person. Subjects in the experiment frequently said, "If it were up to me, I would not have administered shocks to the learner."

I believe that the concept of social metaphysics goes a long way to helping us understand the mentality of the individual who perpetrates cruelties and says "If it were up to me, I wouldn't have done it."

Who was it up to?

It is not ego that opens the door to evil. It is the abdication of ego.

A Retreat to Feelings

When independent, critical thought is suspended, *feelings* may become our sole experience of sovereignty. Our only independent sense of self may become our emotions, even though the chief emotion may be anxiety. Let us imagine entering the psyche of such a person.

"This much I know to be true: I am afraid. The feeling is mine and mine alone. It is not an affectation, not something summoned to impress anyone, but a true expression of my identity.

"At three o'clock in the morning, when I am without an audience and there is no one to approve of me or disapprove, I may know that I am more than the 'reflected appraisals' of significant others, and the world is more and often different from what those others say it is. I may not know this as a conscious, reasoned judgment but as a nameless feeling flashing its feeble signal through fog.

"If I do have snatches of wisdom, moments of lucidity when I see the world through my own eyes, it is often by courtesy of a sub-

conscious intelligence within me that performs connections and integrations outside the net of my subservience; it sends its signals in the form of emotions and feeling-laden thoughts my mind does not always know what to do with. It is hard to know when my inner signals are the product of subconscious rationality and when they are the reflection of my own distortions. It is hard to know when I am seeing things clearly and when I have merely substituted my own delusions for the delusions of others. I am told by some to 'trust my intuition,' but my intuition is sometimes right and sometimes wrong; its reliability is uncertain. I am told by others that my faculty of reason should aid me in this struggle, I should learn reality testing, but who am I to think? Who am I to judge? Who am I to decide? And what if people disagree? I am a stranger and afraid in a world I never made."

When this is the state of consciousness in which we live, the tendency is to understand self-expression and self-assertiveness solely in terms of acting on our feelings in defiance of our authorities. If we concede reason to these authorities, as so often happens, then we frame the issue in terms of emotion versus reason, or instinct versus intellect. It would be an enormous step toward autonomy to question whether one's authorities are in fact exponents of the reasonable and, further, to grasp that in this struggle reason is our ally, not adversary.

Remember that reason is the process of grasping relationships, of integrating our experience in accordance with the law of noncontradiction. Since contradictions cannot exist—since nothing can be true and untrue, a fact and not a fact at the same time and in the same respect—to arrive at a contradiction is to have made an error. However, reason as a process should not be confused with what some group of people at some moment in history might regard as "the reasonable." Some people call "reasonable" preposterous notions that have no basis in reason at all but are merely tradition: since people have always done this, it is reasonable for you to do it. Does such an argument hold water? Clearly not. Example: People have always had slaves, therefore it's unreasonable for you to protest the institution of slavery. Or women have always made themselves subservient to their husbands, so be reasonable and go along with it.

This is what is wrong with that alleged bit of wisdom of George Bernard Shaw that writers so often love to quote. Shaw wrote: "The reasonable man adapts himself to the world; the unreasonable one persists in trying to adapt the world to himself. Therefore all progress depends on the unreasonable man." This is supposed to be profound and witty. But is it reasonable to adapt ourselves to the world? Not necessarily, not if our world is mad. Is it unreasonable to try to adapt the world to ourselves? By no means if our vision is rational. It is social metaphysics to believe that the social consensus is always reasonable and opposition to it always unreasonable.

The point is that social metaphysicians struggling toward some measure of autonomy need to ally themselves with reason against what others are calling reasonable. Then they have a chance for a real breakthrough. But if all they have of their own is *feelings*, they stand on very weak ground. And they know it, which is why they feel so vulnerable, so uncertain, and sometimes so helplessly belligerent.

The importance of feelings here—and they *are* important—is that they can reflect perceptions and integrations taking place outside explicit, verbal consciousness. They must not be ignored or dismissed. They need to be examined to learn whether they offer a pathway to valuable information or are merely a product of distortion and misinterpretation. All of us have felt things passionately that proved to be mistaken. All of us have felt things passionately that against all belief to the contrary turned out to be right. Reason and reality testing are the ultimate arbiters. Abandon them and we have no compass.

If we believe, however, that others have an access to reality superior to our own, we are inclined to concede that theirs is the voice of reason, leaving us—where? We cannot hope to survive or operate effectively in the world guided by nothing but our inchoate emotions. So, sooner or later, we are thrown back into dependency, into reliance on the beliefs and judgments of others. And in despair we conclude that our revolts against social metaphysics are doomed and that we have no choice but to live our lives secondhand.

Working with social metaphysics in psychotherapy, I begin with the importance of listening to inner signals, examining feelings for what they have to teach. This is a vital aspect of cultivating autonomy. But for the enterprise to be successful, an alliance must be formed between feeling and thinking, emotion and reason, intuition and logic.

The typical response of a certain type of social metaphysician trapped in a "people" frame of reference is to ask, *"Whose reason?"* The only answer possible is that it is the responsibility of each of us to exercise our own and to be willing to live with the consequences of our judgment.

It is worth mentioning that one of the worst crimes of our educational system against young people is that principles of critical thinking are not part of every school curriculum. No one should be allowed to graduate high school who has not been trained to recognize logical fallacies. If our aim is to equip young people for independent survival as adults and nurture self-responsibility, what is more important than teaching the appropriate use of mind?

I will have more to say about how we reclaim our autonomy in the process of examining what self-responsibility means when applied to the key areas of life. Additionally, in the Appendix I include a program I developed to assist in the process of attaining a higher level of individuation. In this chapter my purpose has been to illuminate what self-responsibility and lack of self-responsibility entail in the basic operations of mind itself, and to spell out some of the consequences for character development when responsibility is avoided.

When we choose to live mindfully and honor our own perceptions, we create a self who is at home in the universe. When we retreat from this responsibility and transfer to others the task of thinking and judging, we create a painful inner void we then look to others to fill. We live in alienation from ourselves and from reality. The reward of self-responsibility is that *we become a person.*

4

A Self-Responsible Life

I said
earlier that we are responsible for our life, well-being, and actions in all those areas open to our choice. Here, we will focus on what the chief areas and issues are, and what a self-responsible life looks like.

We will consider what the challenges or difficulties might be in operating self-responsibly, what the benefits are, and, when relevant, what the ramifications are for our relationships with others.

One reason it can be helpful to break the issue down into different aspects of life is that we may operate self-responsibly in one context and passively in another. For example, we may be self-responsible financially but dependent emotionally. We may be proactive when working for ourselves but reactive and nonaccountable when working for someone else. We may take a good deal of responsibility for our physical health while taking none for the effects of our irrational behavior with our children or spouse. It would be simpler if we could say of someone that he or she was or was not a self-responsible human being, but reality is more complex than that. Almost always, we have to specify the context. In what contexts is this person self-responsible? In what contexts not?

Although inevitably there is overlap, for purposes of this discussion I propose the following categories:

> I am responsible for the level of consciousness I bring to my activities.
>
> I am responsible for my choices, decisions, and actions.
>
> I am responsible for the fulfillment of my desires.
>
> I am responsible for the beliefs I hold and the values by which I live.
>
> I am responsible for how I prioritize my time.
>
> I am responsible for my choice of companions.
>
> I am responsible for how I deal with people.
>
> I am responsible for for what I do about my feelings and emotions.
>
> I am responsible for my happiness.
>
> I am responsible for my life and well-being.

We will consider, one by one, what self-responsibility means in these areas.

I am responsible for the level of consciousness I bring to my activities. In any given situation, we have options concerning the level of consciousness we activate. We can give full attention, half-attention, zero attention, or any degree along the continuum. Whatever the choice, we are its cause. This, as I discussed in Chapter 2, is the essence of our free will.

The implication is that when I am working on a project, listening to a lecture, playing with my child, talking with my spouse, deliberating whether to have another drink, reading my performance review, wrestling with a personal problem, driving my car, *I am responsible for the level of consciousness I bring to the occasion.*

When and if we confront this fact explicitly, and especially if we accept accountability, we live more mindfully. But often there is resistance to doing so. Some people feel that the disadvantages of operating more consciously outweigh the advantages. This becomes clear when we conduct sentence-completion experiments to explore our attitudes.

Having worked with people in many cities throughout North America as well as abroad, I want to report the kind of considerations sentence-completion work brings to light. For example, I give people the sentence stem "If I bring more consciousness to my daily activities—" and ask them to keep repeating the stem with a different ending each time. While I receive a great many positive responses affirming the benefits of mindfulness, here are typical negative ones, distilled from hundreds of sessions:

I'll have to work harder.

People will expect more of me.

I'll realize how much I hate my job.

Suppose I make a mistake.

I won't be able to play ignorant.

I'll have to correct problems when I see them.

I'd have to call some people on their mistakes, and they might resent me.

I won't be able to goof off.

I'd feel too responsible.

I wouldn't have fun.

I give the stem "The bad thing about living more consciously is—" and I hear such concerns as:

I'll see too much.

I'd have to change my life.

My marriage would fall apart.

I'd have to look at how much I dislike some of my friends.

I'd have to work harder.

My boss would start asking more of me.

I'd have no excuse.

I'd have to confront how much I disagree with my family's values.

When I want to illuminate the self-defeating consequences of persisting in unthinking patterns, I give a stem such as "If I continue to operate semi-unconsciously—" and the same people who gave the kind of endings listed above typically respond:

My life is never going to get better.

I'm digging my grave deeper.

I won't respect myself.

There's no hope.

I hate looking at myself in the mirror.

I'll go on feeling depressed.

I'll always be trapped.

What's the point of anything?

Experiences such as these, repeated many times, confirm my conviction that at some level *people know what they are doing* when they avoid consciousness, think minimally, and constrict their awareness. We may feel sympathy for some of the fears that motivate them. No one can deny that living consciously compels us to confront some painful choices. But in no way does that minimize the fact that we are responsible for the level of consciousness at which we function or that our choices have consequences for the quality of our existence.

Whatever the short-term disadvantages of thinking may appear to be, sight has greater survival value than blindness, and a life lived consciously has more joy and fulfillment than one lived unconsciously. I have known many people who regretted marrying semi-unconsciously; I have never known anyone who regretted marrying consciously—that is, by giving thought in advance to what they were doing. I have known many people who regretted not being more thoughtful when they were raising their children; I have never known any who wished they had been more unconscious. I have known business executives who cursed their lack of thought during a time of crisis; I have never known any who regretted being as clear-minded as possible. I have known salespeople who wished they had given more thought to their customers' communications; I have never known any who wished they had given less. I have known sick men and women who wished they had paid more attention to their body's signals when they were younger, I have never known any who regretted being keenly respectful of those signals. One of the goals of psychotherapy, as I see it, is to evoke an experience of these truths.

Again, let me emphasize that when I say that I am responsible for the level of consciousness I bring to any situation, I am not saying that my control over my mind is unlimited. For example, someone may press me for a decision at a time when I know I am exhausted and not confident that I can think clearly. I am able to say, "I will not decide today. I don't trust myself at this moment." In other words, I may not be able to produce the ideal state of consciousness on demand, but I can know what my present state is and act accordingly.

In psychotherapy we sometimes teach people to say, "I don't choose to speak right now. I'm too angry (or upset or agitated or whatever). Let me cool down a bit."

We can learn to recognize when our state of mind is appropriate or inappropriate to the demands of a situation. And if our judgment says our state is inappropriate, then we need either to change it or to defer taking action. Either choice expresses self-responsibility.

But if we take actions that require clear consciousness when we know consciousness is impaired, we are responsible for the consequences of our actions. To give an extreme example: If we hit and kill someone while driving our automobile in a state of intoxication, the fact that we were drunk is not a moral defense. It is a *worse* indictment than if the accident had happened while we were sober.

As to the consequences for others when a person takes responsibility (or avoids it) for living mindfully, ask yourself these questions: Do I want to work among people who operate at a high level of awareness or the opposite? Would I wish to have been raised by parents who were conscientiously thoughtful about what they were doing with me or parents who were reacting thoughtlessly and impulsively? Do I wish to be married to someone who loves consciously or someone who loves from inside a perpetual mental fog? Do I want to live in a community of thinking human beings or among people whose goal is to get through life with as little thinking as possible?

Whoever accepts the responsibility of thinking, whoever chooses to operate consciously, creates a better world for everyone with whom he or she interacts.

As to the effects of living consciously (or the opposite) on our own sense of competence and worth, let us remember what we have noted earlier: Namely, that for our species the mind is our basic tool of survival. This being the case, nothing is more essential for self-esteem and successful adaptation to reality than valuing sight over blindness and consciousness over unconsciousness.

I am responsible for my choices, decisions, and actions. I am the cause of my choices, decisions, and actions. It is I who chooses, decides, and acts. If I do so knowing my responsibility, I am more likely to proceed wisely and appropriately than if I make myself oblivious of my role as source.

Nothing is more common in moments of acting irrationally than to blank out the awareness that *we* choose to do what we are doing, as if the action were somehow happening of its own accord. This is one of the reasons why people sometimes get drunk or take mind-altering drugs. "I am not responsible—I was out of my mind at the time." But of course we *are* responsible for choosing to intoxicate ourselves.

If we stay aware of the fact that we are responsible for our choices, decisions, and actions, we are far more likely to choose, decide, and act in ways that will not later become causes of embarrassment, shame, or regret. We are not dissociated from our behavior; we are anchored in reality; we see more clearly and tend to function more wisely.

Yet if we wish to take actions that full mental clarity cannot sanction, then there is a temptation to dim awareness, disown responsibility, and alienate ourselves from our own behavior. In this state, we weaken the sense of the connection between ourselves and our actions. *We submerge the knowledge of ourselves as source.*

Consider, for example, the realm of sex. Our sexual choices express deep aspects of who we are, including our unresolved conflicts. Sex is very far from being merely physical, even when we think that is all it is. Just as we can run from confronting pieces of our own soul, so we can disown their expression in our behavior: We can commit an action and tell ourselves, "This is not me." We can disconnect from our most personal and revealing encounters, denying their significance even while feeling compelled to repeat them. Sex is an arena in which we can express ourselves in the most eloquent ways and yet disavow responsibility for doing what we are doing. We summon the fog of dissociation and alienation to protect a false notion of self.

"I have slept with several hundred women," a client, Lawrence M., age forty-seven, an investment banker, once said to me, "and most of the time I was not there." He had come to me because he had never had a truly intimate relationship in his life and knew intimacy frightened him. "I don't think of myself as a promiscuous person, and yet . . . I didn't even like most of the women, let alone feel close to them. I felt, it's not really me doing this."

"And if," I asked, "when you were with them in bed, you had chosen to say to yourself, 'I am responsible for choosing this woman and for being here with her now. . .'?"

"More often than not, I wouldn't have been there. It wouldn't have happened. It all would have felt too embarrassingly stupid. I suspect I would have despised myself."

But he said this almost too facilely as if, even now, he was dissociated from the reality of what we were discussing, still running from any sense of personal responsibility.

I looked at him silently, then spoke with slightly exaggerated slowness, and I saw his breathing subtly deepen as he leaned forward a bit and for the first time that day became fully present to our interaction.

"So, in order to do it, you had to detach from the awareness that it was you who was choosing to do what you were doing?"

"Yes. Had to make that awareness unreal."

I repeated the thought deliberately. "Had to disown responsibility for sleeping with women you didn't much care for?"

"Well, obviously I wasn't thinking of it in these words, but—yes. Of course, it doesn't work. Afterwards, the bad taste is still there."

"Realizing that," I said, "I wonder what you'll choose to do. I wonder what decisions you'll make."

"I guess you're pushing for self-responsibility right now. By not offering any advice. By putting those questions to me."

"Exactly."

The reality of unconscious motivation should not blind us to the reality of choice. To recognize that our behavior is motivated and that often the roots of our motivation are unconscious does not mean that we are not responsible for what we do. As clients in therapy learn to raise the level of their consciousness in regard to their actions and to acknowledge their role as source of those actions, they learn to operate more effectively and less self-destructively—quite apart from what they may or may not come to understand about their deepest motives.

I do not wish to imply that understanding is irrelevant or unhelpful, merely that it is not necessarily a precondition of change.

The more conscious Lawrence became of his accountability for his sexual behavior, the more "spontaneously" he began to exercise better judgment, to be more discriminating, and to feel conscious disgust when he failed to be. He became increasingly eager to dissolve the barrier that resisted a genuine connection with a woman.

Elsie M., age forty, came for therapy because on several occasions she had been unfaithful to her husband, whom she claimed she did not want to lose. Her husband had discovered her infidelities, and they were now trying to resolve their problems. Her infidelities always happened when she had been drinking.

I wondered aloud whether drinking might be a way of avoiding responsibility for her actions.

"I believe," she answered, "that I should have a right to drink when I want to. And to flirt a little. But men are predatory. They don't respect a 'no.'"

I asked her to talk about what she felt drew her to these encounters, and she shrugged and said something vague and noncommittal. Then I asked whether she thought she did anything to convey to men that she was sexually available, and she demanded angrily, "Are you attacking the victim?"

I told her that I was attempting to understand the situation and that I wondered what I was saying that sounded to her like an attack.

What became progressively clearer as we talked was that she had no conscious experience of any responsibility for the problem. She spoke of her actions as if she were discussing an inflamed appendix—troublesome, to be sure, but in no way within the sphere of her own choices or decisions. Any suggestion on my part that volition could be involved activated annoyed defensiveness in her. While professing a desire to resolve the problem of her continuing infidelity and save her marriage, she chose to focus on the inappropriate aggressiveness of men at parties, with the implication that she was the victim of male sexuality.

When I attempted to explore the problem by means of sentence-completion work, she refused to cooperate, stating that the process was too "artificial." After a few more frustrating and nonproductive sessions, we terminated therapy by mutual consent. Later I learned that she consulted a brilliant female psychotherapist and never came back after their third meeting.

Elsie was utterly invested in the vision of herself as a helpless victim. In regard to her sexual behavior, she professed to be responsible and accountable for nothing. She embraced powerlessness as one embraces a life belt in a stormy sea, except that this was a life belt guaranteed to drown her.

That unconscious forces were at work in her was beyond question. That she did not *wish* to be more conscious was also beyond question. She did not wish to understand herself, nor to confront her fear of self-examination, nor to acknowledge that she had any area of power or responsibility in this matter whatsoever. In order to solve her problems, psychotherapy was inarguably needed. In insisting that she was defaulting on an opportunity for self-responsibility, I am not suggesting that all she had to do was to "snap out of it." But without some minimum commitment to accountability on her part, the work could not even begin. In denying all responsibility, she ensured that her troublesome behavior would continue, that there could be no hope of it stopping until she was prepared to say, "These are *my* actions, and I take responsibility for them."

What is significant is that at some level she knew that if she wished to persist in her behavior, she would have to cling to unconsciousness and non-responsibility. Or, to say it in a positive way, at some level she knew that if she cooperated with therapy enough to raise the level of her consciousness of her sexual behavior and force herself to acknowledge some responsibility for her choices and actions, *it would be much more difficult for her to continue as she had been.*

I am convinced that Elsie had the power to give far more to therapy than she chose to give, because over the years I have worked with many clients who initially exhibited her kind of resistance to the process of therapy and subsequently overcame it. They made abundantly clear to me, through sentence-completion exercises and regular conversation, that they carried within themselves the knowledge that, as one man put it, laughing as he spoke, "If I started owning my actions and taking responsibility, that would be the beginning of the end. That's why I fought starting." I am convinced that one of the most helpful things we can do for people is to refuse to buy into their inappropriately restricted views of their limitations. Successful therapy often consists of assisting people to appreciate that they know all kinds of things they think they don't know and can do all kinds of things they think they can't do. It is not compassionate to accept at face value their protestations of powerlessness.

While I have used sex as an example in these two stories, I think it is obvious that the principles involved apply to any arena of human choice and action.

I might be asked, Are there no genuine areas of powerlessness in clients? Of course there are—in all of us. That is why therapy consists of more than simply declaring, "Oh, pull yourself together." But therapy progresses by locating the denied or disowned power bases within us and building from there. There is always *some* point of unused power. Therapeutic exercises aimed at raising consciousness or activating greater self-responsibility, such as sentence-completion work, different forms of psychodrama, and guided fantasy, are intended to stimulate powers within the client that exist but are ignored, undiscovered, or repudiated.

Let us shift from sex to a different problem that many of us can relate to: food. People who overeat are often counseled to eat slowly, consider each piece of food before putting it into their mouth, chew it thoroughly, and then pause before taking another bite. Overeaters often gulp their food, barely taste it, and eat it in a kind of trance that typically lacks consciousness or sense of personal responsibility. The counsel to eat slowly and chew each bite is aimed at breaking down that pattern and breaking the compulsive automaticity of the act. Rarely is this strategy enough by itself to solve the problem, but some clients report that it helps significantly.

One man in a therapy group said eloquently, "I realized that when I gulped my food, tasting nothing, *I* was not there. Awareness, ego, responsibility had all disappeared. Here was an activity that could look piggish from the outside, and yet—

where was my 'I'? Gone, vanished. As I learned to take responsibility for what I ate, something happened apart from losing weight. My sense of self expanded, as if my ego had carved out new territory, saying, 'This space is mine!'"

I had never heard anyone explain more lucidly what I mean when I say that in a sense we create our selves through what we are willing to take responsibility for.

To shift to yet another sphere of human activity, I recall sitting many years ago with a therapy group and reflecting on certain participants' lack of clarity or precision in their comments as well as their seeming *indifference* to clarity and precision of expression. Nothing was different about this session except that for some reason I was especially aware of a lack of focus in some of the statements I was hearing, not from everyone, but from a few people. I wondered if I might be overreacting.

On an impulse, I suggested we go around the circle working with the incomplete sentence stem "If I took responsibility for every word I utter—." It was a stem that had never occurred to me before. I was curious as to what I might learn.

Here are some endings that were later transcribed from a cassette recording:

I'd have to be in much higher mental focus.

I'd have to speak more clearly.

I'd be afraid of having my words judged.

I'd reveal too much of myself.

I'd have to be conscious.

I'd be scared to open my mouth [laughter].

I might be taken more seriously.

I'd be accountable for the quality of my communications.

I could be held to my words.

I'd have to operate at another level, mentally.

I would be clearer.

I wouldn't say stupid or hurtful things.

I'd have to be more honest.

This exercise seemed to energize the group and give their comments more purpose. Excitement in the room rose. The group agreed that if, while speaking, they were more conscious of themselves as the *source* of the words coming out of their mouths, the quality of their communications would be transformed.

"But one would need to be so *focused*," someone protested, "*so aware.*"

The oldest person in our group, a man in his sixties and the father of three sons, became sadly thoughtful and said, "I don't know, I'm remembering some of the incredibly cruel things I said to my boys when they were growing up . . . ways I lost my temper, went berserk when I was frustrated . . . and the scars I left, as my father left scars on me with his outbursts . . . and it would have been impossible to talk that way, impossible, impossible, if I took responsibility for what I was saying while I was saying it. But who would think of such a thing?"

The impulse to disconnect from or actively avoid responsibility for one's actions can show up in any aspect of life. I am thinking of a CEO who consulted with me recently. Fred M. owned a rapidly growing insurance benefits company that he loved and was deeply proud of. His complaint was that he had little capacity for leisure. "I would love to goof off sometime, but you can't imagine how hard it is for me to allow it." He knew that his work-focused way of living was excessive and unhealthy, and in the long run not good for his business either. "I need more balance in my life. I know that. But I resist it."

I asked him to consider what he might do if he were willing to make the solving of this problem as conscious a purpose as signing a new client. He immediately reworked his schedule on a notepad in my office to allow time for "goofing off."

After we talked for a while about the difficulties he might encounter in putting his plan into action, he remarked, "It's suddenly hitting me that with all my complaining, I have never before taken serious responsibility for solving this problem. I've just complained."

Then he volunteered an impressive insight. "And I'm seeing something else. In the past, when I had gone on working too long without a break, when my body was screaming for some leisure that I wouldn't allow, *I solved the problem by getting sick.* Then I had an excuse to stop and rest. I couldn't help it. It wasn't my fault. That's what I could tell myself. I didn't want to be the one who decided that I should take a break. So I passed the buck to my body. 'It's not me who decided, it's my damn body that let me down.'"

I said, "You didn't want to take responsibility for choosing to take off a day or two, or go on a vacation."

"Yes, yes. I didn't want to be responsible. So I conned myself into believing I was merely the victim of a cold or whatever."

"How easy or difficult do you think it will be for you to change?"

"I like your idea of making this project my conscious purpose. That's business talk, and I understand that. Let's see if I can learn to take pride in treating myself better. It's like playing chess against old voices in my head saying 'Mustn't stop working, mustn't stop, mustn't stop.'"

Some years ago, while lecturing at a university, I met George T. A twenty-three-year-old African-American psychology student who had been arrested as a teenager and prosecuted for looting and burglary. His lawyer had won an acquittal by arguing that George was the victim of a bad environment and racial discrimination—in effect, that "George couldn't help it."

I was struck by the intelligence of the questions this young man asked me after my talk, and we sat outside on the campus lawn for a while, and he told me his story.

"Ever since that acquittal," he said, "I've felt bad, humiliated. I didn't know what was bothering me until I heard your lecture today, just knew I didn't like what had happened, though I was glad not to go to jail, but today I got it . . . got what's been eating me for the past six years. *I don't like—I've always hated—being identified as a victim.* It's demeaning. You're not a human being, you're a victim of society. I want to say: I knew what I was doing—I chose to do it—I could have chosen otherwise—other guys chose not to steal and loot—*I am responsible.*"

"Why do you want to say that?" I inquired.

"Because it's the truth. And because it reclaims your dignity." Then he corrected himself: "It reclaims *my* dignity."

"Sounds like you've done a lot of thinking these past few years."

"All I know is, seeing myself as a victim . . . didn't have a father, one brother's in prison, another's a crackhead, poor me . . . blaming everybody else just means same ol' same ol'. My lawyer said, 'What way out did he have?' Bullshit. What about the people from my background who get out without stealing? That's what I was thinking about during your lecture. And how different your message is from the messages I hear in classes here. If you know you're responsible for your life, you find ways. Sooner or later, you find a way."

"A lot of people don't want to know they're responsible," I said.

"Sure, but you don't help them by telling them they're right. You don't encourage them to take more of the crap that's killing them."

I could not help but feel how wonderfully unpredictable life can be; that I should hear such observations coming from a student with George's background. An ex-thief was displaying a more profound grasp of psychology and morality than did many of the professors at the institution where he was studying.

If I may permit myself a lighter note on which to conclude this section, I would like to offer some examples of denial of responsibility for one's actions while driving a vehicle. These are actual words of drivers that appear on automobile accident forms, published by the Arizona Safety Association.* I hope their humor does not detract from what they disclose about the evasion of responsibility.

- "Coming home, I drove into the wrong house and collided with a tree I don't have."

- "A pedestrian hit me and went under my car."

- "The guy was all over the road. I had to swerve a number of times before I hit him."

- "I had been shopping for plants all day and was on my way home. As I reached the intersection, a hedge sprang up, obscuring my vision. I did not see the other car."

- "As I approached the intersection, a sign suddenly appeared in a place where no stop sign had ever appeared before."

- "An invisible car came out of nowhere, struck my vehicle, and vanished."

- "The pedestrian had no idea which direction to run, so I ran over him."

- "The indirect cause of this accident was a little guy in a small car with a big mouth."

---

*See *The Oz Principle,* by Roger Connors, Tom Smith, and Craig Hickman.

- "The telephone pole was approaching. I was attempting to swerve out of the way when it struck my front end."

No one would feel safe on the road if most people behind the wheel lived by the philosophy implied in the above statements. Could any of us feel safe in a world where most people lived by such a philosophy?

Setting aside the humorous aspect of these statements, it's worth thinking about whether (or to what extent) we say things of an equivalent nature when excusing or justifying our own actions.

I am responsible for the fulfillment of my desires. When we are very young, we naturally look to our parents to fulfill the role of caretakers. We announce our desires in the hope that our parents will satisfy them. As children, we take it for granted that others should provide for us a new toy, for example, or money to go to the movies.

As we grow to adulthood, most of us learn that *we* are responsible for the fulfillment of at least some of our desires. Most of us learn that if we desire money, we need to earn it. If we desire food, clothes, or a new car, we need to earn the money to acquire them. An adult who never learns this lesson is considered immature, because we associate financial dependence with childhood and youth. Grown-ups are expected to be self-supporting.

But of course we have many desires beside financial ones. For example:

I want to be happily married. Do I believe it is someone else's job to make me happy, or do I take responsibility for doing whatever is within my power to achieve the result I desire? Do I think about what a happy marriage requires? *What am I willing to do to get what I want?*

I want to resolve the quarrel I have with my spouse. Do I wait for my spouse to make the first move, or do I exercise initiative in seeking to achieve a resolution? *Do I pout, or do I think and act?*

I want to raise happy, self-confident, self-responsible children. Do I assume that if I follow my "heart," my good intentions will be sufficient? Or do I study the subject, perhaps read what is available in the literature on child-rearing, or make some other effort to learn what is known about effective parenting? *How much energy am I willing to expend?*

I want to be a writer (or a scientist or an entrepreneur). Do I daydream about it, or do I *work* at achieving the goal? Do I give thought to what I will need to learn and master, or do I merely talk about my aspirations? *Do I have an action plan? Am I implementing it?*

Often the achievement of our desires depends in part on the participation and cooperation of other people. No matter what I do, for instance, I cannot have a happy marriage without the cooperation of my partner. But the question is: Am I doing everything within my power? Do I take responsibility for doing what is up to me? If I want to run an effective office, and for that I clearly need the active participation of others, then taking responsibility does not mean attempting to do *everything* myself. I have to know what is up to me and what is not up to me.

If I have a goal that requires the participation and cooperation of other people, I have to respect their self-interest. This means that I have to offer values that will be meaningful and motivating. No one exists merely to serve me.

A self-responsible leader or manager does not say, "What is wrong with people that they do not perform better?" Rather he or she asks, "What must I do to inspire people to give me their best?"

A self-responsible salesperson does not complain, "People are so suspicious and skeptical!" Rather he or she asks, "What must I do to win the trust and confidence of my clients and customers?"

One of the most common causes of frustration and unhappiness is people's fantasy of a rescuer who will someday materialize to solve their problems and fulfill their wishes. This is why in my work I am always stressing that *no one is coming*. No one is coming to save me; no one is coming to make life right for me; no one is coming to solve my problems. If I don't do something, *nothing is going to get better*.

The great advantage of fully accepting that no one is coming is that it puts power back in our own hands. *We are through with waiting and free to act.* As long as I am overempowering others, imagining only someone else can save me, I am disempowering myself. In my avoidance of self-responsibility, I condemn myself to passivity and helplessness.

It does not take much to see that men and women who take responsibility for the fulfillment of their desires live better and experience more satisfaction than do those who attempt to pass that responsibility to others.

As for the social consequences of taking responsibility, again I ask: Who would we rather deal with, those who are passive or those who are proactive in their pursuit of their desires? Who would we rather marry? Work with? Welcome to our community?

And how consistently do we treat the fulfillment of our wants as *our* responsibility?

I am responsible for the beliefs I hold and the values by which I live. This means, first of all, that we acknowledge *ownership* of our beliefs and values—that is, that we recognize them as *ours*. This presupposes a reasonable degree of self-awareness. Many of us are utterly oblivious of the premises behind our actions. We unconsciously harbor ideas about the opposite gender, for example. We may act on impulse and feel little need to understand the roots of the impulse. If we do not practice self-reflection or self-examination, we cannot live at a very high level of consciousness. So it is very difficult for us to take responsibility for our beliefs and values. We experience them, in effect, as given.

The responsible individual in this sphere strives to make beliefs and values conscious so that they can be critically scrutinized and so that he or she can be more in control. Unfortunately, many people's upbringing or education fails to teach them the importance, or even the possibility, of this process.

We are all, of course, aware of *some* of our beliefs and values. Let us focus on these here. If we live by premises we have accepted or adopted passively and unthinkingly, it is easy to tell ourselves that these premises are just "my nature," just "who I am," and to avoid recognizing that choice is involved. In contrast, if we are willing to recognize that choice and decision are crucial when beliefs and values are adopted, then we can take a fresh look at our premises, question them, and if necessary revise them. Responsibility sets us free.

For an extreme example of lack of self-responsibility, consider a married woman with three children who comes to therapy complaining that she is unhappy and unfulfilled. "I did everything I was supposed to do," she says. "I picked the kind of husband my parents could approve of. I learned how to be a good wife. I read all the books on parenting. I'm the perfect hostess. I'm active in charities. *So why do I have fantasies of killing someone?* I feel so betrayed. I was told: If you follow the rules, you'll be happy. So I followed the rules. *But I'm not happy.* I want to blame my parents. I want to blame the whole world. *I feel like such a victim. Life is so unfair.*"

For an example of taking proper responsibility, consider another way that she could describe this problem: "I wanted my parents to love me. I wanted to be popular. So I adopted the values my family offered without giving them any independent thought. I chose to let others think for me. That way I thought I'd always 'belong.' Now I'm confronting the fact that their values don't work for me, don't bring me satisfaction or fulfillment. The truth is, my parents' taste in men isn't mine, and I never especially wanted to be a mother, and my life bores me. I don't know what my options are at this point, but that's what I want to explore. I want to start taking responsibility for my life. I want to *think* about my values. I've never chosen to do that before."

Few of us seem to enjoy being asked to account for why we believe and value the things we do. It does not take much probing to discover that much of the time we are merely reflecting what others believe and value—the problem of social metaphysics. Or else our ideas seem to be born out of our feelings and "instincts," for which we cannot adequately account. We are comfortable only with people whose feelings are like our own and uncomfortable with those whose feelings aren't.

When I give clients the sentence stem "If I took responsibility for my beliefs and values—" here are some typical endings:

> I'd have to think about them.
>
> I'd have to treat ideas seriously.
>
> I would question a lot.
>
> I'd know how confused I am.
>
> I would throw away a lot.
>
> I'd be in conflict with my folks.
>
> I don't know what would happen in my marriage.
>
> I would really have to examine things.
>
> I'd have fewer judgments, but I'd be more sure of them.
>
> I would think more clearly.
>
> I wouldn't be so quick to draw conclusions.
>
> I'd ask, "Why?" a lot.
>
> I'd be a different person.

If we recognize within ourselves the problem of social metaphysics, the way out requires that we learn to take responsibility for our beliefs and values. It is essential to assert ownership of our own mind. As the above sentence endings show, the simple act of taking responsibility shifts us (if only briefly) from secondhand consciousness or dependence, to firsthand consciousness, from dependence to sovereignty, because in that instant our primary relationship is to reality rather than to other people's beliefs about reality. We can see in these endings selves struggling to be born.

Whether or not social metaphysics is involved, for those who want to work on autonomy and self-responsibility in the sphere of beliefs and values, the program I offer in the Appendix will be helpful. It is intended to facilitate outgrowing social metaphysics but is not confined to that issue: It is designed to be useful to anyone who aspires to greater independence and individuation.

I am responsible for how I prioritize my time. Time is the most basic currency of life and often the most abused. The temptation is to treat time as an enemy, disowning our need to make choices, *for which we are responsible.*

Our choices and decisions determine whether the disposition of our time and energy reflects our professed values or is incongruent with them. A woman may insist, for example, that her children are her highest value but spend far more of her time shopping with her friends, playing cards, or playing golf, than she spends with her children. A man may declare that his most important priority at work is participating in the development of new products, while 90 percent of his time is devoted to office trivia that produce zero income. These contradictions must be examined. Are these two people deceiving themselves about the nature of their values? Or are outside factors obstructing the translation of their values into appropriate action? If we are clear in our understanding that how we prioritize time is our choice and our responsibility, then we are more likely to address and correct the contradictions than if we tell ourselves that we are somehow victims of circumstances. *Taking responsibility is the key to finding a solution.*

When business consultants visit a firm, they often ask executives to list their (professed) priorities in one column on a page. Then in an adjoining column they record how they actually spend their time. Often there is no match between the two columns, which can come as an embarrassing shock. The next step, which is often the hardest, is to persuade these executives to take responsibility for the discrepancies, to recognize them as an expression of *choice.* Sometimes, of course, discrepancies are unavoidable, due to unforeseen emergencies. But by definition this is the exception, not the rule; if it is the rule, the discrepancies cannot be defended by claiming unusual circumstances. Either the real priorities are not what they are professed to be, in which case rethinking is necessary, or the executives involved are insufficiently purposeful in keeping themselves on track, which also necessitates rethinking. In either case, *the contradiction is their responsibility to resolve.*

When I give executives the stem "If I take responsibility for how I prioritize my time—" the endings I typically hear include:

I would have to say "no" more often.

I'd eliminate about 30 percent of what I do.

I'd be more productive.

I'd enjoy work more.

I wouldn't allow people to distract me.

I'd delegate and then leave people alone.

I'd see how out of control I am.

I wouldn't routinely accept responsibility for solving problems that other people try to pass off on me.

I would see to it that the most important things got done *first*.

This is a useful sentence stem for all of us to explore. Every day for a week, write, "If I take responsibility for how I prioritize my time—" at the top of a fresh page and write six to ten endings for it. It is an educational experience. And it tends to generate change.

Mastering the disposition of one's time (to the extent that this is within one's power) is essential to living self-responsibly.

I am responsible for my choice of companions. Veronica J., age thirty-four, was a dental hygienist whose lover of seven years was repeatedly and almost compulsively unfaithful. "If only Stan would come to therapy," she complained, "but he won't. What's the matter with men, anyway?" When I asked her when Stan first gave evidence of infidelity, she said that almost from the beginning she caught him in flagrant lies about his relationships with other women. She wept and suffered but never seriously challenged his behavior. Her constant refrain was, "Everything would be so wonderful if only he would change." It was several difficult months of therapy before she was willing to take responsibility for *choosing* Stan for a mate and for *choosing* to remain with him and to sanction his behavior. The next step in her progress was to give him an ultimatum: Stop his flings and seek professional help, or the relationship would end. When she saw that he refused to take her ultimatum seriously, she left him. "It's agony," she admitted to me. "I still miss him. The good thing is, I don't feel like a victim. I feel like a grown-up—in charge of my own life. I chose to enter a relationship with Stan, in spite of what I knew about him. I chose to remain, in spite of what he did. And now I've chosen to leave. There are no victims in this situation." The refusal to be a victim, in situations where real choices do exist, is one of the meanings of self-responsibility.

The sentence stem "If I take responsibility for my choice of companions—" typically elicits such endings as:

> I wouldn't be in some of the relationships I'm in now.
>
> I'd get out of some of my friendships.
>
> I'd say "no" more often.
>
> I'd be more discriminating.
>
> I'd admit what I feel about some people.
>
> I'd more more careful about what I agree to socially.
>
> I wouldn't blame people for being who they are.
>
> I'd hold myself accountable for choosing to remain in a relationship that hurts me.

The stem "If I deny responsibility for my choice of companions—" typically elicits such endings as:

> I keep getting into stupid situations.
>
> I complain about others and never look at my own role.
>
> I get to feel sorry for myself.
>
> I avoid facing my problems.
>
> I'm always waiting for the other person to make things right.
>
> I cry, "Life isn't fair!"

I wonder if I'll ever be happy.

I get into lousy relationships.

I sentence myself to being passive and helpless.

If we examine and reflect on these endings, they speak for themselves. They tell the whole story.

Here are a few more examples worth pondering:

"If I took responsibility for my choice of companions," a participant said at a seminar, "I couldn't possibly sleep with some of the people I've slept with."

"If I took responsibility for my choice of companions," said another, "I'd have to face what my real values are—as opposed to what I say they are."

"If I took responsibility for my choice of companions," said another, "I'd start looking for a job so I could afford to leave my spouse."

Naturally many of us find it tempting to avoid the kind of responsibility I am describing. The advantage is that then we do not have to take action. We can suffer, feel sorry for ourselves, and blame others. And we can fulfill a subconscious life script that tells us pain is our destiny. The disadvantage is that then we are stuck in our unhappiness, defeated and disempowered, all our power granted to anyone but ourselves. Yet the power is there, waiting to be taken. *The price is to recognize and own our choices.*

I am responsible for how I deal with people. This is already entailed by the recognition that we are responsible for our choices, decisions, and actions, but I want to focus on it separately here because it deserves the emphasis.

Whatever I choose to say or do, I am the author of my behavior. I am responsible for how I speak and how I listen. I am responsible for the rationality or irrationality of my dealings with others. I am responsible for the respect or disrespect I bring to encounters, for the fairness or unfairness, the kindness or unkindness, the generosity or meanness. Whether I choose to speak to others' intelligence, or to pander to their vices, it is my choice. Whether I keep my promises or break them, it is my decision.

If I support my child's dignity, I am responsible for the act of doing so. If I slap my child's face because I dislike the noise he makes while playing, again I am responsible.

We try to avoid responsibility when we declare, "He or she *made* me do it." These are the lies that people use to justify their cruelty: "She got on my nerves." "He drives me crazy." "It was her fault I—" "I wouldn't have done it if he hadn't—"

If we are adults and no coercion is involved, other people do not control our actions. In most situations we have choices about how we will respond. But if we do not wish to recognize these choices, we tell ourselves and others that we were not responsible, that we had no choice and were *compelled* to act as we did.

I am responsible for how I deal with my child, spouse, neighbor, friend, client, associate, customer—*any person I encounter.* An act of choice is always involved. The only question is: Am I willing to be accountable? My answer to that question says a good deal about my stature as a human being.

I am responsible for what I do about my feelings and emotions. When we act on the basis of a feeling or an emotion, we often believe that what we did was more or less inevitable, that the feeling or emotion determined our behavior. We may be unaware or we may not wish to be aware that a choice or decision was involved. We find ourselves saying:

I felt angry, so I smacked my child.

I felt hurt, so I withdrew and stopped talking to my mate.

I felt afraid, so I turned down the job opportunity.

I felt sexually attracted, so I slept with my spouse's best friend.

I felt impatient, so I drove my car recklessly.

I felt envious, so I told a malicious story about my colleague.

I felt jealous, so I made wild, senseless accusations to my wife.

The truth is, none of these feelings *necessitated* the actions that followed. Not everyone who experiences these emotions handles them like the people in these examples.

If we are educated to understand, or manage to learn on our own, that we are responsible for the actions we take on the basis of our feelings, the chances are that we will be less impulsive and more thoughtful about our behavior. But if we operate on the implicit premise that whatever impulse hits us must be followed, if we believe that feelings are to obeyed without judgment, then we become reckless drivers through our existence. And to disown responsibility, pleading "I couldn't help it," alters nothing—except, perhaps, by degrading our stature still further.

Few people would argue against the desirability of all of us taking responsibility for what we choose to do about our feelings and emotions. It is self-evident that our lives and the world we help to create would work better. But we are unlikely to see widespread acceptance of self-responsibility in a culture strongly influenced by intellectual leaders who celebrate emotion above reason and impulse above judgment, and who endlessly justify people's irrationality by their powerlessness in the face of feelings. It is imperative that we become acquainted, or reacquainted, with the reality of *choice*.

"Have you ever," I ask clients, "wanted to do something desperately, and yet not done it?" Of course clients answer yes. I ask, "Have you ever felt a powerful impulse and yet not acted on it?" Again clients invariably answer yes. "Have you—*often*—recognized the necessity of exercising discrimination and judgment about what you will do or not do?" Yes. "Then you already know—by your own experience—that you have choices about what you do about your feelings. So we cannot really disclaim responsibility, can we? We can pretend, but who are we deceiving except ourselves?"

"The trick," one client said to me, "is to stay conscious of this truth in the moment of action."

Exactly.

I am responsible for my happiness. I began this book with a discussion of the relationship between my happiness and my self-responsibility, and so I will be very brief here.

If I take the position that my happiness is primarily in my own hands, I give myself enormous power. I am not waiting for events or other people to make me happy. I am not trapped by blame, alibis, or self-pity. I am free to look at the options available in any situation and respond in the wisest way I can. If something is wrong, my response is not, "Someone's got to do something!" but "What can I do? What possibilities exist? *What needs to be done?*"

If I take the position that my happiness primarily depends on external events not in my control, I relinquish my power. My responses to life are passive and reactive. I may resent those who fail to make me happy. I may hate my parents, my spouse, my friends, my colleagues, all of whom have deeply disappointed and betrayed me. Still, I secretly imagine that if I suffer enough, perhaps *someone will come.*

When I give clients the sentence stem "If I take more responsibility for my happiness—" I hear these endings:

I wouldn't suffer so much.

I'd do things differently.

I wouldn't wallow in pain.

I'd let my parents off the hook.

I'd think about what would bring me happiness.

I'd pursue my goals.

I wouldn't blame other people.

I wouldn't keep screwing up to torture my mother.

I wouldn't just sit in my apartment.

I'd admit it when I *am* happy.

I wouldn't self-sabotage.

I'd speak up about things I don't like.

I'd say "yes" to the things I want.

I'd be more active.

My clients are often astonished to realize that they have more control over the level of their happiness than they thought. Not that they are omnipotent or completely unaffected by external realities, but they do have a range of options for how to respond. They do have choices. This discovery, if and when it is fully accepted, tends to be exhilarating.

I am responsible for my life and well-being. This idea undergirds everything I have been saying. In one respect, it is deceptive. It is not as simple as it may appear. Not many people would want to argue with the desirability of this approach—in the abstract. The difficulties arise when we make all its logical implications specific and concrete.

Who would dispute, for instance, that it is evidence of maturity for an individual to take responsibility for his or her life and well-being? Is this not what we encourage in psychotherapy? (Unless one is a "radical" therapist who encourages the belief that the root of personal problems is society and that mental health begins with the insight that one is oppressed.) And yet many therapists who champion self-responsibility in their consulting rooms also campaign for social programs that turn citizens into wards of the state.

If we embrace self-responsibility not merely as a personal preference but as a philosophical principle, logically we commit ourselves to a profoundly important moral idea. In taking responsibility for our own existence, we implicitly recognize that other human beings are not our servants and do not exist for the satisfaction of our needs. We are not entitled to treat other human beings as means to our ends, just as we are not means to their ends. We are not entitled to demand that others work and live for our sake, just as we do not work and live for theirs. We are each of us ends in ourselves. Morally and rationally, we are obliged to respect one another's right to self-interest.

This idea is inherent in our Declaration of Independence. Ours was the first government *ever* to recognize and affirm the inalienable rights of the individual. It upholds (in principle, though not always in practice) the idea that the individual belongs not to the state or the nation or the society, but to him- or herself. The life, liberty, and happiness that one is guaranteed the freedom to pursue are one's own.

In the history of the world, this was a new idea. And its battle for full acceptance is far from won.

A consistent application of this principle would lead us to the following rule of human relationships: *Never demand that a person act against his or her self-interest as he or she understands it.* This means that if we wish people to take an action or provide value, we are obliged to offer reasons that are meaningful and persuasive in terms of their own interests and goals. Morally, we may not coerce them to violate their own judgment in obedience to our commands. Force is permissible only in retaliation against those who have *initiated* its use. In normal human dealings, that which we cannot obtain by another's voluntary consent *we are not entitled to.* Legally, we require people to honor the contractual commitments they have chosen to make, to protect the rights of the other party, but we do not tell people what commitments to make.

The principle of voluntarism and of respect for individual rights is the moral foundation of mutual respect, goodwill, and benevolence among human beings. It rejects the notion that some people may be treated as sacrificial fodder for the goals of others, which is the premise underlying all dictatorships and almost all political systems, with the exception of libertarianism. (See *Honoring the Self.*)

If one wishes to observe seemingly reasonable men and women become hot under the collar and lose a good deal of their coherence, I suggest the following experiment. Find a psychologist who is an advocate of self-responsibility when counseling clients and an advocate of the welfare state when dealing with politics—a type of person not at all difficult to find. Such an individual will be very clear about the impropriety of a client demanding self-sacrifice from family or friends—and also quite vehement about everyone's right to "free" medical care, housing, and so on, *which someone else has to produce.* Inquire as to how this contradiction is to be reconciled. Unless one already shares the same orientation, one will not be impressed by the logic of the answers one receives.

Not that this behavior is peculiar to psychologists. I mention my own profession because I am so often struck by its inconsistencies.

My observations are not meant to argue against mutual aid or social cooperation. There are plenty of good reasons for people to choose to help one another in times of difficulty. And Americans have a long tradition of doing so—voluntarily.

What I argue against is the doctrine that one is born with a "right" to the mind, work, and energy of other human beings, and that the coercive apparatus of the state is allowed to enforce this claim.

It is in the nature of things that any one of us may need help from strangers at some point in our lives, but self-responsible people do not demand it as their due. They appreciate it as an act of generosity. They do not imagine they were born holding a mortgage on the energy and assets of other people, although plenty of politicians and intellectuals tell them otherwise.

Today the attitude of entitlement has reached epidemic proportions. A *Time* magazine journalist characterized our current too prevalent attitude as follows: "If I want it, I need it. If I need it, I have a right to it. If I have a right to it, someone owes it to me. Or else I'll sue." This short statement condenses the antithesis of self-responsibility.

We will return to this subject in Chapter 8, when we discuss a culture of accountability.

From the Personal to the Political and Back Again

We have seen that the idea of living self-responsibly has many applications and ramifications, from carrying one's weight in a marriage to acknowledging authorship of one's actions to earning one's living.

One aspect of the intimately personal that I want to consider next arises in the domain of child-parent relationships. Let us now consider the challenge of separation.

5

The Challenge of Separation

When a person enters psychotherapy, we sometimes embark on an exploration of childhood history. The purpose of such an inquiry is not to affix blame for any difficulties the client might be experiencing but to understand the historical context in which the client developed.

We look at such issues as the values and beliefs to which the child was exposed and may have internalized; the way the child was treated and the conclusions he or she drew from that treatment; the view of him- or herself the child was (implicitly) encouraged to hold; any significant life experiences that represented special challenges to the child's development, such as physical abuse or sexual molestation; any other unusual events that may have influenced the child's view of life.

In other words, what was the environment to which the child had to adapt and what kind of survival strategies did the child learn that may still be operative today?

We know that children learn coping strategies that may have some usefulness when they are five or six, such as being very quiet to avoid punishment or very compliant to win approval and protection, that later on become not only obsolete but dangerous to the well-being of the adult. In T. S. Eliot's play, *The Cocktail Party*, a psychiatrist says to the leading character, "You are nothing but a bundle of obsolete responses." In therapy, we want to know where those obsolete responses originated. What were the circumstances that made them seem necessary and desirable?

We want to build a platform of self-awareness and self-understanding on which an individual can learn to take responsibility not only for the resolution of specific problems, in partnership with the therapist, but also for his or her long-term well-being.

No part of the therapeutic agenda as I conceive it is to persuade the client that someone else is to blame for his or her problems. Neither is the client encouraged to self-blame. Rather the client is taught to substitute for the question Who's to blame? the question What needs to be done?

One of the goals of therapy is to clear the way for the independence and self-responsibility of an adult mode of functioning.

Two Forms of Dependency

At the extreme, there are two seemingly opposite kinds of clients. The first finds it difficult to say anything bad about their parents; the second finds it difficult to say anything good. The first sees the influence of parents as entirely positive; the second as entirely negative. When discussing personal shortcomings, the first vehemently denies that parents could have made any contribution to present difficulties; the second vehemently insists that parents are entirely responsible for present difficulties. The first sees his or her parents as saints; the second as monsters.

Neither type finds it easy to look at their parents realistically. In different ways, both appear overly tied to their child-hood and overly dependent on their parents.

I recall a client whom I treated nearly twenty-five years ago, Eric H., a young man of nineteen, here from England, study-ing political science at UCLA. He was excessively shy, rigid, so-cially inhibited, with the appearance of being emotionally tortured. Eric described his mother and father as warm and loving and his childhood as idyllic.

The exaggerated intensity with which he did so made me curious. One day I proposed that I hypnotize him and do some exploration of his earlier years with the hope of better understanding his difficulties, and he agreed. When I re-gressed him to the sixth year of his life, Eric began to weep and, in response to my question as to what was happening, de-scribed a scene of being savagely beaten by his father. He went on to describe several such scenes between his fifth and eleventh years. He then spoke of being the target of much ridicule from his mother. When I asked about his emotional response to these experiences, he spoke in an anguished voice of feeling humiliated, demeaned, powerless, and enraged. He insisted that he had to keep all his feelings hidden. The image his parents were intent on communicating to everyone was that of a perfect family.

I was aware that if Eric had blocked out these memories all these years, he must have felt he had good reasons for doing so—defenses exist to serve a purpose—and I did not want him to feel overwhelmed when he awakened from the trance. So I said that there was no need for him to remember *right away* anything from this session he did not feel comfortable remem-bering and that I had confidence in the wisdom of his subcon-scious mind to let these memories surface *in the right way and at the right time.*

"I guess I can't be hypnotized" were his first words when he awoke. With a handkerchief he wiped his face clean of tears without any apparent awareness of what he was doing. We chatted for a few minutes, and he seemed irritable and angry with me.

Then, without any context, he demanded, "Won't you admit that there are some wonderful parents in this world?" I answered that of course there were and then I inquired what prompted the question. Instead of answering, he launched into a passionate speech about the kindness of his mother and father and the happiness of his childhood years. He looked at me defiantly.

When he returned a week later he asked if we could attempt hypnosis again. I interpreted this to mean that he was now ready to confront the threatening material he had described while in a trance. We went through the same material again but in considerably more detail, and again I ended by saying that he did not have to remember anything *yet* that he was not *feeling* comfortable remembering, thereby implying that he could remember it a later date.

This time, however, when Eric came out of the trance he remembered everything and said in a desperate rush, "That's the way it *really* was, so awful, you cannot believe, I was suffocating and frightened, and I'm still frightened, because if I admit all this, if I make it real . . ." He stopped talking and gazed off, as if he had gone back into trance and were contemplating a series of internal pictures. I remained silent and waited. The session ended uneventfully, with nothing further of significance being said.

At our next meeting I proposed we do a sentence-completion exercise. I told Eric not to worry whether any of his endings were particularly significant or profound. Any grammatical completion of the stem would do. We agreed to tape-record the session because I suspected I would want him to listen to it later, before his next session. (Today, almost all my clients tape-record their sessions.)

We began with the stem "All my life—," and his endings included: "I've been unhappy; I've been trapped; I've wanted love; I've been afraid of what people would see when they looked at me; I've not wanted to make mistakes; I've wanted my parents' respect and support; I've wanted their lies to be true."

When I heard this last ending, 1 gave a new stem: "If I could make myself believe my parents' lies—." After repeating it before each ending, Eric said, "I tried but I couldn't; I was going crazy; I could make them really love me; I would be their perfect son; I wouldn't be alone."

This inspired the stem "If I weren't afraid of being alone—." He ended with: "I wouldn't be me; I could live; I wouldn't feel humiliated all the time; I could believe in myself; I wouldn't have to play the good boy."

Then Eric stopped and made one of those great leaps that provide some of the most thrilling moments in psychotherapy. He said to me, "If I were willing to be responsible for my own life, if I didn't believe I somehow needed my parents' support for my survival—I don't mean financially, I mean *spiritually*—I could look at my childhood and see it for what it was."

I was reluctant to speak, because I wanted him to stand in the presence of his own statement. We remained silent through a long moment. Then I said, "Sounds like you've hit on a pretty important realization. . . . I imagine it's difficult, growing up . . . without any belief that you're capable of handling your own life . . . without much appreciation of your own resources . . . feeling you somehow need your parents' blessing and approval to survive and function . . . yet never really feeling you've got that, either. . . . It must be hard."

I knew that at this moment what was most important was for him to experience his pain and sense of powerlessness. We cannot transcend what we have never confronted. Self-responsibility cannot begin until one is willing to look at reality. Or, more precisely, the choice to do so is the first act of self-responsibility. Later Eric would build on that foundation, learning to evolve from a child's state of consciousness to an adult's.

I knew that the process had begun when, very timidly, he said, "Yeah."

In contrast to Eric, Alan J., age thirty-nine, a physician, seemed to remember every injustice that had ever been perpetrated by his parents against him and was eager to talk about them. It seemed that his father, who had emigrated from the Ukraine at the age of twelve, had been a clothing merchant who worked fourteen hours a day and spent much of his spare time playing cards with relatives. He was not disposed to participate in Little League with his son or hold fatherly conversations with him, except to tell him from time to time that he was stupid, especially when Alan manifested his inability to master poker or even to be interested. With indignation he recalled his father saying, when Alan was sixteen, "God, you're so skinny. When I was your age I could have broken you in two." Alan had an older brother and sister, but it was he who his mother chose as her confidant and spent endless hours complaining to Alan about his father or about Alan's worthless brother and sister or about some relative who had slighted her "because," she told him, "you're the smart one of the family." Often when Alan wanted to read, his mother would call to him to sit on the porch and listen to her talk of life's disappointments. Alan said he felt despised by his father and overcontrolled by his mother.

I first met Alan when he attended a weekend self-esteem seminar I conducted. During the first day, we did a number of psychological exercises aimed at exploring significant childhood experiences. Alan left the session feeling anger and indignation at his parents. This was not my intention or the point of the exercises. I learned next day, Sunday morning, that the previous evening he had confronted his seventy-six-year-old mother and berated her for her cruel treatment of him. I had the impression that his uneducated mother did not understand the meaning of many of the psychological terms he was using and was bewildered by the entire diatribe. Alan reported she began to weep and to insist that she had done the best she could, which only inflamed him more. "You didn't make me feel *visible!*" he shouted. He said he would have liked to make the same scorching speech to his father, but he had died some years before.

I regretted that this was how he had chosen to apply our work, and I pointed out that whatever his parents' shortcomings might have been, the problem was now within him and had to be solved internally. It was much too late to dream of reforming his parents. I did not think my communication was successful.

After that, I did not see him for nearly a year. He came to therapy when his wife of ten years left him after announcing that he was a self-pitying, self-indulgent baby blind to anyone's feelings or needs but his own. He was devastated. How could anyone possibly see him that way, he demanded of me, since he worked as hard as he did and since his patients idolized him?

His wife, with whom I spoke once, informed me that on one occasion when she had threatened to leave him, he had flung himself on the floor and began pounding his fists and weeping.

If he wasn't a good husband, he said in therapy, it was because his father was a bad role model. If he complained excessively, while being unresponsive to his wife's feelings or needs, that was how he saw his mother behaving, and she must have influenced him. If he was sometimes cruel and insensitive, that was because his parents never made him feel lovable. Didn't experts agree that children who are not loved tend not to feel lovable? He was his parents' son, he declared. How could anyone expect him to be somebody else?

I was sure, I told him, that he knew better responses than his were possible, and I was sure that he would like to learn them.

Not very enthusiastically he answered, "Of course."

That this thirty-nine-year-old man still experienced himself as a child was obvious. That his parents, one of whom was dead, still remained the most important figures in his life was also obvious. By insisting that he was his parents' creation psychologically, not merely biologically, and that his behavior was irresistibly shaped by his parents' behavior, he created a trap for himself from which he saw no escape.

If a man like Eric illustrates one form of dependency, a man like Alan illustrates another. They are dependent in different ways, but they are both dependent. They both reflect inadequate separation and individuation.

The Problem

The issue Alan presents is one aspect of the territory we are exploring. What does self-responsibility entail when one is working through psychological problems whose roots in some sense seem traceable to noxious childhood experiences?

It is, after all, an indisputable fact of reality that many children are raised in extremely nonnurturing environments, environments hostile to normal development. It is a fact of reality that children can be ignored, rejected, humiliated, abused, molested, subjected to violence, and tormented in any number of ways.

And yet when people are encouraged to see themselves as victims, the danger is that they will remain stuck in passivity and in the belief that only other people (or perhaps a higher power) can rescue them. If, implicitly, we teach people victimhood as their core self-identification, we are not teaching self-responsibility. We are teaching dependency and impotence. The danger is that they will feel "Someone's got to do something!" and that if the rescuer does not come, they are doomed. The world is full of people who are waiting for Godot.

Confronting the Past

When I began practicing psychotherapy nearly four decades ago, my basic orientation was cognitive. I understood psychological problems primarily in terms of mistaken or irrational beliefs—I called them "premises"—that were driving the client down a self-destructive path. Emotions were of interest principally because of the underlying premises they revealed. Childhood was of interest principally as the context in which faulty premises were originally formed.

Over the years I learned that to solve most of their problems, my clients needed a way of working that was deeper and more comprehensive, engaging the subconscious as much as the conscious and the emotions as much as the intellect. Consequently, my work became increasingly experimental and experiential, addressed to all parts of the psyche, not just the conscious mind. In its initial stages, this "opening up" of my approach is obvious if you read *The Disowned Self,* written three years after the publication of *The Psychology of Self-Esteem.*

In my early work my focus was almost entirely on "the timeless present," where premises naturally reside. However, my clients soon forced me to see that if I was to be effective, I would often (not always) need to spend more time exploring the life circumstances in which a self and its strategies originally developed. Furthermore, I saw that the exploration had to be *an experience* and not an intellectual exercise. Some of my more academically oriented clients could describe the most appalling childhood incidents in the manner appropriate to a lecture on higher mathematics. But this behavior is not confined to professional intellectuals: Truck drivers are as capable of disassociating from painful life experiences as anyone else. In other words, it is possible to talk about personal events without ever allowing them to become fully real to oneself. Psychologically, we keep the reality of what happened at a distance to avoid suffering.

I saw that so long as this remains the case, we can talk endlessly without any healing or change occurring. Painful feelings that are fully confronted and experienced tend to dissolve through a process of integration, whereas feelings that are disowned persist and continue to cause difficulties.*

In the case of clients who had frightening or traumatic early experiences, I wanted them to feel the reality of what it was like to be a child living through those events, to liberate themselves from self-blame for their parents' hurtful behavior, and to gain perspective on how those events affected subsequent development. I wanted them to understand the *conclusions* they had derived from those events about themselves and about life, as well as the coping strategies they had learned. I wanted them to do all the grieving that was necessary, to be sure, but I also wanted them to *think* and *to take responsibility for the process of recovery*. This last means actively participating in the work rather than leaving all responsibility to the therapist. This active orientation helps to build self-esteem.

But there are clients who grow attached to their pain and fiercely resist the rest of the healing process. They see their experiencing of pain not as a transition stage on the way to recovery but as an end in itself. They see their perception of the injustices done to them not simply as a necessary aspect of self-understanding but as justification for any objectionable behavior of their own. They see therapy not as a launching pad for independence and happiness but as a substitute for living. Their passivity is the only form of "survival" with which they feel safe; they operate within a view of self and the world that makes their policy seem appropriate.

I will not say that alternative possibilities never occur to these clients, never penetrate their defenses, but they usually

---

*Whether healing integration occurs depends, in part, on how the process is framed conceptually; but this a technical matter, beyond the province of this discussion.

brush them aside because they do not wish to know that such possibilities exist. The basic motivation is not a desire for joy but a fear of pain. Anxiety and fear tend to be the controlling influence in their lives.

Megan R., age thirty-one, was an unmarried accountant who had had many years of therapy before I met her. She entered therapy for the first time at the age of nineteen, for depression and difficulties in her relationships, and spent four years lying on a couch free-associating and listening to interpretations of her dreams, without discernible improvement. She remained unhappy, sullen, passive-aggressive, and (as she herself acknowledged) often resentful of happiness or success in others.

A friend persuaded her that she was too emotionally repressed for "talk therapy" to do her any good and that she needed a therapy primarily focused on releasing blocked feelings. For another three years she went twice a week to an institute where, in a padded room with dolls to play with, a nursing bottle to suck on, and a crib to lie in, she was encouraged to scream out her repressed pain. For the first time, she confessed that at the age of eleven and for several years thereafter, she had been sexually molested by her father, and that for a long time her mother refused to believe it. In therapy she was encouraged to relive incidents of molestation many times and as vividly as possible. Her therapist congratulated her for reaching a point where she cried deeply at least once a day. "You're feeling your feelings," he informed her. But she was still unhappy.

Eventually, disenchanted, she left her therapist and a few years later found her way to an incest support group where she was helped to understand that *of course* she was depressed and her life did not work because she did not adequately understand that she was a victim. Pain was not enough, she was told; she needed to learn rage—rage at her father for what he did. She learned to express hatred for both her parents.

This group was the best experience she'd had, Megan said to

135

me, except that she had been going for a very long time and she was still miserable. "When does grief work end?" she wanted to know. "When is the 'inner child' healed?" She asked it not like a thirty-one-year-old woman but like a forlorn waif who cannot understand the universe's lack of compassion. She wondered aloud if she should forgive her parents and turn her problem over to God.

Throughout of all of her therapeutic experiences, as far as I could learn, no one had ever suggested to Megan that she bore any personal responsibility for the course her life took *as an adult*. The focus was either on the injustices that had been done to her or the pain she was experiencing. That these awarenesses were necessary was undeniable; they contributed to the process of healing. But by themselves they were not enough; they would not launch anyone's self-esteem.

As an introductory experiment, I asked Megan to keep repeating the sentence stem "If I choose to operate five percent more self-responsibly—," and put different endings to the sentence each time. Her endings included: "I'd have to pay more attention to what I do; I wouldn't mope; I'd think more about what I want to do; I'd stop dwelling on what's wrong with everybody else; I'd stop dreaming of my father begging my forgiveness; I'd be more interested in life; I wouldn't make what happened an excuse for all my fears."

Then I gave her the stem "If I were to breathe deeply and feel my own power—," and her endings, which illustrated one of her basic conflicts, included: "I would like that; It would make me uncomfortable; I would let go of pain; I would be free; I would be frightened; I would be on my own then; I would know Mother isn't going to save me; I would have to be a grown-up; I would wonder how to live; where would I find the strength?; I would respect myself."

Then I gave the stem "The good thing about clinging to the past is—," and she ended with: "I don't have to grow up; I can blame my parents; I have an excuse for everything; it isn't good, I'm tired of clinging to the past."

I gave her the stem "The good thing about seeing myself as a victim is—," and she ended with: "I *was* a victim; I can wait for grown-ups to solve my problems; I can imagine Mother and Father facing what they did and making amends; I can make them guilty; I get revenge; I don't have to challenge myself."

To the stem "The bad thing about seeing myself as a victim is—," she responded with: "What does it get me?; it just leaves me with no place to go; I'm miserable; I'm sorry for myself; I'm a baby, and I'm sick and tired of it; I want to be more than a victim; there's more to life, isn't there?"

Blame and Forgiveness

There is no conflict between conveying compassion for a client's suffering and seeking to evoke in the client a spirit of self-responsibility. There is no conflict between helping the client understand when real injustices have been perpetrated against him or her and discouraging the client from turning victimhood into a self-definition.

Mother and Father may indeed have behaved monstrously. One should not tell a client not be hurt or angry. If I counsel against a focus on blaming, it is not to protect the parents but to protect the client. A preoccupation with blaming leaves the blamer disempowered. "You made me what I am today—I hope you're satisfied!" Blaming is a dead end. What is needed is a focus on solutions, which entails discovering one's own resources and mobilizing the will to use them.

If I am not an advocate of blaming, neither am I an advocate of forgiveness as a necessary prerequisite of well-being. If the offense has been so great that the client feels he or she never again wants to deal with a parent (for example, a father who subjected the client to repeated incidents of physical violence),

I do not argue. What I advocate is that the offense be *accepted*, which is not the same thing.

To accept is not necessarily to like, admire, condone, or forgive. It is to experience the reality of what happened without denial, disowning, or cries of "Why did you do this to me?" (which is still a form of protesting reality). To accept is to refuse to fight unalterable facts. To accept is to be willing to stand in the presence of truth without looking away, moralizing, arguing, or otherwise attempting to escape. The goal of acceptance, in this context, is to *let go* of pain, resentment, and over-absorption with the past. In other words, to separate and move on.

But when therapists under the influence of certain religious teachings insist that not only must the client accept that it happened but must also *forgive* the offending parent under all circumstances, regardless of the nature of the offense or the parent's attitude and behavior today, then this can be a demand that the client do violence to his or her own consciousness. Forgiveness may require major repression.

Perhaps we should ask, What does it mean to forgive? Does it mean that the offending actions did not take place? But they did. Does it mean that their impact was not hurtful and destructive? But it was. Does it mean that the client has come to believe that, at the time, the parents were doing they best they could, so there are no valid grounds to fault them? But while this is sometimes true, it is not always or necessarily true.

If what is meant is that the client has learned to let go of anger over the past, which would be healthy, it is confusing to label this development "forgiveness." In my experience, the point at which many clients arrive is one where they feel neither forgiveness nor lack of forgiveness—the concept itself becomes irrelevant—because they do not think in such terms. Their upbringing is no longer a charged issue. Their emotional energies are invested in the present, not the past.

With some parents it is realistic to hope for a happy reconciliation, and this goal should be supported by the therapist. With others the best the client can aspire to is benign indifference or something very close to that. The only general rule I know of that fits all cases is the importance of acceptance— and letting go.

None of this is to deny that if a benevolent relationship with parents is possible, it is desirable. A five-year-old cannot be expected to understand a parent's emotional problems, but a grown-up may be able to. A grown-up may say, "After all, my parents too had parents. Often they were scared and insecure themselves. Or inhibited. Or ignorant. If am able to create a happy life for myself today, why would I wish to go on resenting them for the past and depriving myself of what might be possible between us now?" When a client says something like this, I take it as a sign of maturity. I applaud it, not in the name of forgiving the parents, but because it signals to me that the client is now operating at a higher level of independence.

My only concern is that this attitude be authentic and not faked or achieved by repression. Sometimes it is faked and can be the disguised form of unresolved dependency. The unspoken message to the parents is, "See? I don't hold hard feelings, in spite of how you treated me. Are you appreciating what a good boy (girl) I am? Will you love me and be good to me *now?*" Fear of autonomy wears many masks.

Choice

Parents who wish to nurture self-responsibility in children look for opportunities to offer children choices and options, and encourage them to think through the consequences of their decisions. We know that children are in danger of being infantilized when choices and decisions they are capable of making are too often made for them by others. These truths apply equally to psychotherapy.

When clients are caught between blaming parents for every

current setback versus taking responsibility for their own actions, or respecting their own perception of reality versus obeying the edicts of parents, or between confronting painful feelings versus denying and disowning them, or between telling a difficult truth versus withholding it, or between dealing with associates fairly versus dealing with them exploitatively and autocratically, in every way possible I emphasize the role of *choice.* "'Take what you want,' said God, 'and pay for it,'" is my favorite Spanish proverb. The more we are aware that we *choose* our actions, the more likely we are to take responsibility for them. And learning to take responsibility for our actions is a precondition of taking responsibility for our life.

As clients learn to do this, they continue the process of shaping their identity. When and as they own not only their actions but the choices and decisions behind them, they expand and strengthen the experience of self.

When clients present life problems in a way implying that I should provide a solution, I typically say something like "What options have you considered? What are the pros and cons? What do you think you'll do?" When clients mention behaviors they know to be undesirable but in which they nonetheless persist, I may say something like "What ideas do you have for changing this? What possibilities are you considering? If you made changing this behavior your conscious purpose, what might you do?" When they talk about how badly their parents treated them, at some point I may ask, "What conclusions did you draw from that? How do you think you were affected? What do you imagine you could do to give yourself better possibilities today? If you brought a higher level of awareness to this problem, I wonder what might occur to you. Can we explore that?"

We might move at some point from discussion to a variety of psychological exercises, such as I have written about in *The Six Pillars of Self-Esteem* and other books aimed at shifting clients to a higher level of consciousness, at helping them explore possibilities, dissolve blocks, heal old wounds, break out of false notions of their limitations, and reintegrate splintered parts of the self. But the context in which this work is done is always: Your life is in your hands; you are responsible for your actions and choices. *What do you want to do?*

Blaming, I tell clients, is a pastime for losers. There's no leverage in blaming. Power is rooted in self-responsibility. *What are you willing to do to make your life better?*

More than one client has expressed some form of this thought: "I began to grow, I began to get a grip on my life, when I finally accepted that if I didn't start to do something different, *nothing was going to improve.*"

When Protectors Become Destroyers

When therapists and support-group facilitators fail to communicate this understanding, what we sometimes see as a result is the phenomenon of persons for whom therapy or support groups are a way of life, an endeavor without end. I am thinking of the people who remain with the same therapist or support group for ten, fifteen, or twenty years and are convinced that they could not survive otherwise. They believe that the most important thing about them is their wounds, not their resources. For them, being in therapy or in recovery is what they do and who they are, and we have to assume that they are supported in this attitude by their therapists, group facilitators, and fellow group members.

When one of the most famous figures in the Recovery movement compares "adult children of alcoholics" to Holocaust victims, insisting that their suffering is for all practical purposes equivalent, since both suffer from posttraumatic stress disorder, he is not doing a service to those whose champion he professes to be. In Nazi Germany and the countries it dominated, and in Cambodia, "holocaust" was not a metaphor. It can be very painful to grow up with parents who are alcoholic, but it is offensive to equate that with seeing one's parents, spouse, or children tortured and killed in front of one's eyes and living every day under threat of the same fate. All suffering may need to be respected, but it also needs to be seen in perspective. When it is not, victimhood and self-pity become lifelong identity badges for the converts.

To be sexually molested by a parent or other adult can be a terrible experience. But if therapists and group facilitators convey that the victim is doomed to carry the wound for life, always damaged, then sexual molestation is now being compounded by *spiritual molestation*. In both contexts, persons who should be protectors operate as destroyers. What victims of abuse, sexual or otherwise, need is understanding and compassion, to be sure. But they also need support in appreciating that they are more than their past traumas, more than their problems, and that they have the resources to conquer and grow beyond misfortune. They need to know that they are not sentenced to lifelong incapacitation. They are not helped by being defined in terms of the least resourceful moments of their existence—that is, by those moments in childhood when the abuse occurred.

The most effective psychotherapists are those who know how to mobilize strengths and capabilities that lie dormant within the client. The least effective are those who do not know that such resources exist, those whose ability to see is limited to pain. The tragedy is that they can worsen the problem they propose to cure.

If I was able to help Alan and Megan, discussed above, to move beyond childhood pain and grow toward autonomy, I first had to assist them in fully confronting that pain and then learn to accept and let go, *and to frame this very act as an expression of newfound, self-assertiveness and self-responsibility*. This was accomplished, in part, by the way I set up the assignment. "Are you willing," I would ask, "to go back and look at what the child you once were had to contend with and had to survive? Do you have the strength and courage for that? If so, give yourself credit. There is health and life in you, in spite of anything that happened. You were not destroyed, and you are not going to be destroyed. You can weep and rage—and learn. And out of all that, you can create a new life. If you're willing to summon from within yourself what it will take. If you're willing to fight for that child and for the future that child deserves. This may be the most heroic thing you will ever be asked to do. Are you willing to take on this project?"

I do not wish to oversimplify the complexities and difficulties that may be involved. The road is rarely easy and always frightening. In some form, however, this is the challenge we often need to present in psychotherapy. When we can answer "yes" to it, we are ready to begin a self-responsible life.

I want to shift our focus now from what self-responsibility entails in child-parent relations and consider its implications for man-woman relations. How does one operate self-responsibly in the context of love and marriage?

6

Self-Responsibility and Romantic Love

Some years ago I wrote a book entitled *The Psychology of Romantic Love.* It was written under difficult circumstances. My wife Patrecia had died at the age of thirty-seven in a drowning accident, and I was still in a state of mourning. While embarking on the book—it was now two years after the accident—I was struggling to create a new relationship with my present wife, Devers. I was raw, vulnerable, emotionally chaotic. Never had the subject of love felt more important to me. I felt I was writing in blood.

It was a book I had wanted to write for more than a decade. Its purpose was to project a new view of romantic love and to identify the key factors that are likely to determine the success or failure of this kind of relationship.

Shortly after the book was published, I was interviewed by a newspaper journalist. She asked a number of questions about how I understood the concept of romantic love and what I saw as its challenges, and then she said, "Dr. Branden, if you don't mind, I'd like to raise a personal question. Doesn't romantic love *scare* you?"

Her question was totally unexpected and I was intrigued. "Why would it scare me?" I asked.

She answered, "You're fifty years old. One doesn't expect to hear people of your age speaking so passionately about romantic love. I'm only twenty-eight. I think of so many things that can go wrong—the person leaving you, falling for someone else, or their job taking them away, or else the person dying. It's so frightening. You've already had a tragedy in your life. And now you've begun a new relationship, and you've written this book . . . I don't know where that courage comes from, if that's the right word. I feel I don't want passion in my life, don't want intensity, don't want to go that deep. I guess I value safety more."

I asked, "Do you mean that avoiding pain is more important to you than experiencing joy?"

"Yes."

I answered, "Well, that's a choice, isn't it?"

But she persisted. "And also," she went on, "the way you write about it, love is a big responsibility. It asks a lot of us."

"Yes, it does," I agreed.

"I know this sounds awful," she confessed, "but I'm not sure I want to be that responsible, either."

Romantic Love and the Needs It Satisfies

Let us begin by briefly considering the meaning of love. When we love a person in the most general sense of the word "love," we see in that individual the embodiment of important values of ours, so that we associate him or her in some way with our pleasure, joy, or fulfillment. We want to interact with this person, and we are concerned about his or her well-being. In the absence of such a response, we cannot call the feeling "love." (This last point needs to be stressed because sometimes people say they "love" someone when the truth is that they merely *need* that person and have no interest in the person's welfare

145

apart from how they personally are affected by it.)

Romantic love includes the above but goes further. It demands a response at the highest level of emotional intensity. It places the desire for interaction and involvement at the center of our emotional life. It implies the presence of a strong sexual factor. Romantic love means finding a soul mate—someone whose values and sense of life mirror our own. We feel a drive to organize our life around this person and no one else. When someone says, "I love you" in a romantic context, this is what they are understood to be saying.

Romantic love is a passionate spiritual-emotional-sexual attachment between two people that reflects high mutual esteem. We would not characterize a relationship as romantic love if the couple did not experience their feelings as passionate or intense, at least to some significant extent. We would not describe a relationship as romantic love if there were not some sense of spiritual affinity, some deep mutuality of values and outlook, a deep emotional involvement, or a strong sexual connection. And without mutual admiration—if mutual contempt instead characterized the connection, as certainly happens—again we would not describe the relationship as romantic love.*

What are the basic human needs that love has the power to satisfy? They include the following:

- First, there is our need for human companionship: for someone with whom to share values, feelings, interests, and goals; for someone with whom to share the burdens and joys of existence.

- There is our need to love: to exercise our emotional capacity in the unique way that love makes possible. We

---

*For readers who associate "romantic love" with immaturity and neurosis, I refer you to the book mentioned above.

need to find people to admire, to feel stimulated and excited by, to whom we can direct our energies.

- There is our need to be loved: to be valued, cared for, and
  nurtured by another human being.

- There is our need to experience psychological visibility: to
  see ourselves in and through the responses of another
  person, with whom we have important affinities. This is
  our need for a psychological mirror, one of the most important aspects of relationships.

- There is our need for sexual fulfillment: for a counterpart
  as a source of sexual satisfaction.

- There is our need for an emotional support system: for at
  least one other person genuinely devoted to our well-
  being, for an emotional ally who, in the fact of life's challenges, is reliably *there*.

- There is our need for self awareness and self-discovery: for
  expanded contact with the self, which happens continu-
  ously and more or less naturally through the process of intimacy and confrontation with another human being.

- There is our need to experience ourselves fully as man or
  woman: to explore the potentials of our maleness or fe-
  maleness in ways that only romantic love makes possible.

- There is our need to share our excitement in being alive
  and to enjoy and be nourished by the excitement of another.

I call these "needs" not because we would die without them,
but because we live with ourselves and in the world so much
better with them. They have survival value, physically and spiritually.

I believe that anyone who reads this list can recognize not

merely the reality of these needs but also the hope that through a love relationship they will be fulfilled. These thoughts may not be entertained consciously and explicitly, but they are there, if only implicitly and nonverbally, when we enter the domain of romantic love.

This view of the possibilities of man-woman relationships is relatively new, historically speaking. Romantic love is often attacked today by psychologists, sociologists, and anthropologists, who frequently scorn it as an immature, illusory ideal. To such intellectuals, the idea that an intense emotional attachment could form the basis of a lasting, fulfilling relationship is simply a neurotic product of modern Western culture. Of course they load the concept of romantic love with a good many immature notions and attitudes that make it very different from the concept as I am characterizing it here.

It is true that young people growing up in twentieth-century North America take for granted certain assumptions about their future with the opposite sex, assumptions that are by no means shared by all other societies. These include that the two people who will share their lives will choose each other, freely and voluntarily, and that no one—not family or friends, church or state—can or should make that choice for them; that they will choose on the basis of love, rather than on the basis of social, family, or financial considerations; that it very much matters which human beings they choose and, in this connection, that the differences between one human being and another are immensely important; that they can hope and expect to derive happiness from the relationship with the person of their choice and that the pursuit of such happiness is entirely normal, indeed is a human birthright; and that the person they choose to share their life with and the person they hope and expect to find sexual fulfillment with are the same. Throughout most of human history, these views would have been regarded as extraordinary, even incredible.

Only during this century, especially the second half, have

some of the educated classes in non-Western cultures rebelled against the tradition of marriage arranged by families and looked to the West and its concept of romantic love as a preferred ideal. Although in Western Europe the idea of romantic love (in some sense) has had a long history, its acceptance as the proper basis of marriage has never been as widespread as it has been in American culture. To be sure, individual men and women in every culture and at every time in history have fallen in love; but they were the exception, not the social norm; often they loved in defiance of the social norm. Classical Greece, for example, saw passionate love as a form of madness. As Burgess and Locke write in their historical survey *The Family: From Institution to Companionship,* "It is in the United States that perhaps the only, at any rate the most complete, demonstration of romantic love as the prologue and theme of marriage has been staged."

Why the United States? The answer, at least in part, is philosophical. What was distinctive about the American outlook and represented a radical break with its European past were its unprecedented commitment to political freedom, its individualism, its doctrine of individual rights, and, more specifically, its belief in a person's right to happiness *here on earth.* Both the individualism and the secularism of this country were essential for the ideal of romantic love to take wide cultural root.

Even now—in the midst of the rampant cynicism and despair of the final years of the twentieth century, and notwithstanding the attacks on romantic love by intellectuals—people continue to fall in love. The dream refuses to die. The question is: What is needed to make love work?

In my past writings, I have focused on the fact that self-esteem is essential. The first love affair we must consummate successfully, I have said, is the love affair with ourselves. Only then are we ready for a relationship with another. If I feel unlovable, I will find a way to sabotage my romantic happiness because I will feel I do not deserve it.

Here, I want to focus on another factor that plays a vital role in a successful relationship: the practice of self-responsibility.

Self-Responsibility in Marriage

For the purposes of this discussion, I use the term "marriage" not in the legal sense but in the sense of a seriously committed relationship between two adults who experience the feelings toward each other described above—a sense of affinity, sexual desire, and admiration—and whose intention is to build a life together.

In a general sense, the principles of applying self-responsibility to relationships have already been identified in the chapter entitled "A Self-Responsible Life," but what I want to offer here are some specific applications and elaborations.

I am responsible for my choice of partner. Sometimes men and women experience a strong sexual attraction for each other, conclude that they are in love, and proceed to live together or marry on the basis of their sexual attraction. They ignore the fact that they have few values or interests in common, have little or no appreciation of each other as people, and may be bound to each other principally by dependency. Sometimes when they discover these facts, the relationship falls apart. But are such relationships love? I do not think so. To love someone is to know and love his or her person. Love without consciousness, insight, or knowledge is not love.

Perhaps the first application of self-responsibility in this context is that of truly seeking to see and understand the person with whom we are involved. This demands the willingness to look at reality and to confront relevant facts, whether the process is pleasant or unpleasant. The choice is whether a relationship will develop out of awareness and appreciation or out of need, dependency, and willful blindness.

A woman in therapy once said to me, "Can you imagine it?

Three times I have married men who turned out to be alcoholics—and I never found out until after we were married! Can anyone deny that I'm a miserably unlucky woman? Life is so unfair!"

Contrast that with a statement made to me by a woman (not a client) who said, "An hour after I met the man I married I could have given you a lecture on ways he would be difficult to live with. I think he's the most exciting man I've ever known, but I've never kidded myself about the fact that he's also one of the most self-absorbed. He spends a great deal of time in a private world of his own. I had to know that going in, or else I would have been very upset later. I've never been happier in my whole life than I am right now in this marriage. But not because I tell myself my husband is 'perfect' or without fault. I think there are very few major surprises about the person you marry—if you pay attention from the beginning. Through their behavior, most people announce who and what they are pretty clearly. Trouble is, often we don't care to look. Or we're lost in wishful thinking. Possibly we're controlled by our need or our loneliness. We create a fantasy and then get angry with our husband because he's not the fantasy, which he never pretended to be. But if we're willing to look without blinders, if we're willing to see everything that's there to be seen, shortcomings as well as strengths—and if we still love passionately—that's what I call mature romantic love."

I do not wish to imply that we cannot be honestly mistaken about our romantic choice. Even the most conscious of us can make an error of judgment. Or our partner can change over the course of our relationship so that he or she is no longer the person we originally fell in love with. But this does not make us victims. If we remain in the relationship, we do so by choice.

Sometimes when I hear men and women complain interminably about their spouses, as if their marriage were some kind of natural disaster that happened to them through no action of their own, I ask, "Have you looked at the fact that this is the person you *chose* and are *choosing* to remain with? Are you willing to examine your own values, motives, and payoffs in the situation? If you describe your relationship as intolerable, what are the rewards for remaining in it?"

I once had a friend who I liked in many respects but who had one trait for which I had no sympathy: He was forever complaining about the current woman in his life, presenting himself as the hurt and baffled victim of her irrationality, instability, infidelity, or underdeveloped sexuality. "Have you ever asked yourself why you choose these types and why you choose to remain with them, even after the worst is known?" I said to him one day.

He looked at me gloomily, with only a hint of humorous self-mockery in his eyes, and replied, "Do you suppose it's because my mother always made my life miserable?" Perhaps I should mention that he was not a sensitive intellectual or chronically wounded poet. He was a professional fighter and teacher of unarmed combat, widely regarded as one of the toughest men on the planet. The story has a happy ending, however. He found the resources to heal himself, to stop seeing himself as a victim, and to choose a woman with whom he created a happy marriage. By way of explanation, I think he would say, "I finally grew up."

I am responsible for choosing to accept—or refusing to accept—certain behaviors of my partner. This point closely relates to the foregoing. Naturally, no one is going to like and enjoy everything a partner says or does. And all of us at times choose to put up with behaviors we do not particularly like. This accommodation is both necessary and inevitable in marriage. But having acknowledged this, an essential point remains: We cannot have decent relationships if we do not have some limits on what behaviors we regard as acceptable.

On the dark side, if there is nothing our partner can do that would cause us to protest or leave, no atrocity that would be too much for us to tolerate, we have neither marriage in any sane sense nor self-esteem, but only some form of mindless bondage. Different people draw the line in different places, but everyone needs some concept of the unacceptable. Everyone needs to make a judgment about what is tolerable and what is not. Self-esteem demands it.

If we put up passively with sarcasm, verbal abuse, exploitation, or physical violence, we are responsible for our decision. If we make our partner's life miserable by complaining about every triviality, we are responsible for that as well. Our standards may be wise or foolish, rational or irrational, but we are responsible for them and we need to own this fact.

A self-responsible individual is willing to stand by his or her judgment and to be accountable for what he or she deems acceptable or unacceptable.

A woman I knew was unhappy with her husband because he did not earn a higher salary. She told him he was immoral not to be more ambitious, although he had never presented himself as having high monetary aspirations and seemed perfectly contented with the life of a high school teacher. I asked her if she would be willing to say (without turning it into an abstract moral issue) that she was unwilling to remain married to a man who did not earn more money and that his attitude and policy were personally bothersome to her. She was reluctant to do as I asked. She did not want to make the matter personal. Her form of avoiding self-responsibility was to dress up her preferences in the language of morality. She did not want to confront the naked statement, "I want a husband who earns more money." She said, "Putting it that way would make me sound too materialistic."

"It's not a sin to want more money," I observed, encouraging her to own her desire.

"But don't you think he would be much happier if he got out of teaching and into the real world?" she asked.

My point is not that our moral standards are never relevant

to our assessments of our partner's behavior. Sometimes they obviously are—for example, if we learned that our partner was embezzling funds from an employer. But we need to be aware of the temptation to avoid self-responsibility by concealing personal preferences behind high-sounding ethical or religious abstractions.

I am responsible for communicating my wants. In romantic love, the presumption is that the wants of each partner matter to the other—matter more, in fact, than to any other person with whom our relationship is less intimate. But there is a responsibility on which many men and women default. They do not send clear signals concerning their desires. As a result, their partner does not respond as hoped for. And then there may be hurt feelings and resentment.

One form of avoiding self-responsibility, then, is expecting our partner to be a mind reader. Why does this happen so often in relationships?

When one or both people in a relationship complain of not having their wants respected, I often give them a sentence-completion exercise. They face each other, and one does a string of sentence completions aloud to the other: "One of things I want from you and rarely get is—." This provides an easy channel through which to articulate their longings and frustrations. This is usually followed by the stem "One of the ways I make it difficult for you to give me what I want is—." The goal here is to raise consciousness concerning their possible contribution to their own frustrations. The endings I hear most often include:

I don't tell you what I want.

I act like I don't want or need anything.

I'm always giving to you and make of my giving a wall you can't get through.

I find fault with whatever you try to do for me.

I act indifferent.

I pretend to be totally self-sufficient.

Of all these endings, the most common is "I don't tell you what I want." This inspires the stem "The good thing about not telling you what I want is—." "The good thing" is a way of eliciting underlying motivation. Here are typical endings:

I won't have to find out whether you care or not.

I don't have to deal with the fear of rejection.

I don't feel I have a right to wants.

I get to feel like a martyr—that's my role.

Stems aimed at drawing out the reasons behind the other self-sabotaging behaviors, such as acting indifferent or super-critical, elicit similar endings. In clients' responses, two themes predominate: fear of rejection and fear of not being entitled to any desires or needs of their own, both of which are clearly self-esteem problems.

One way of working on our self-esteem and simultaneously working toward the solution of this relationship difficulty is *to take full responsibility for naming our wants and being certain that the partner hears and understands.*

There are no guarantees that someone who loves us will always satisfy our wants. But we will certainly achieve more satisfaction than if we keep our desires a secret. To express our wants may not guarantee fulfillment, but to suppress them does guarantee frustration.

What if we are afraid to speak our wants plainly? We acknowledge the fear to ourselves and to our partner. We describe our apprehension simply and honestly. And then we communicate our wants. It does not serve our interests to be stopped by fear of being hurt or to participate in romantic love while telling ourselves that we have no right to personal desires.

We have a responsibility to treat ourselves with the respect we hope to receive from others. Otherwise, when seeking love we ask for a contradiction.

I am responsible for how I choose to respond to my partner's expressed wants. If my partner expresses the desire that more of our leisure time be spent alone together rather than with friends, I may choose to discuss this desire or act as if I had not heard it; to acquiesce, or disagree, or propose a compromise; to treat it seriously or flippantly; to respond benevolently, angrily, defensively, or indifferently. If my partner expresses the desire for some particular kind of vacation, a way to spend a Sunday, a new item of furniture, dinner at a particular restaurant, some activity, or a personal favor, all the same options confront me, and I am responsible for how I respond.

If we love someone, it seems natural to want to respond affirmatively to his or her desires, although obviously it is not always possible to do so. But one of the ways love is expressed is through the bias being on the side of *yes*. And if this observation is valid, then we clearly have a responsibility to be *conscious* when our partner communicates wants and *conscious* of how we respond. We need to be aware that we are making a *choice*.

Working with couples, what often strikes me is how oblivious they can be of the fact that a choice is involved. Their responses are often cognitively passive—that is, devoid of thought—and therefore lacking in any internal sense of responsibility. They are insensitive to the fact that such moments and issues create the character of a relationship.

When I wish to open this matter in therapy, I sometimes give the sentence stem "If I were to treat my partner's wants with respect—" and I hear such endings as:

I'd have to really listen when my partner speaks.

I'd have to think about what she (or he) is saying.

I'd be much kinder.

I'd take the time to explain when I can't do what I'm asked to do.

I wouldn't "forget" what I'm asked so often.

I'd be treating my partner seriously.

I'd be treating the relationship seriously.

I'd say "yes" or I'd say "no"—consciously and responsibly.

I sometimes recall with amusement an incident that happened many years ago in therapy. I was counseling a couple who seemed very devoted to each other. The wife's complaint was that they made love only when her husband initiated it. If she attempted to initiate, he almost always declined, claiming not to be in the mood. It would have been easy to interpret their problem as a struggle for control, with the husband refusing to yield control by responding to his wife's overtures. But after listening to them for a few minutes and observing the flow of their mutual affection and respect, I doubted this explanation and suspected that something much simpler might be involved. I made the observation that relationships seem to work best when both parties make a genuine effort to say "no" to their partner as rarely as possible. The husband said, "In principle I agree with you. But sex is different. I mean, what am I to do if I'm reading the paper, or just sitting in a chair thinking about some subject, and Donna comes over, starts kissing me, indicates that maybe in the next hour or two, if not right away, she'd like to make love? A man can't be expected to just throw a switch and suddenly be ready for sex, can he?"

I laughed, and asked, "Why not? Millions of women do that every day." As he stared at me in bewilderment, I went on. "Do you believe that by some incredible marvel of synchronicity every time you're feeling amorous and your wife responds, she was already thinking of sex and in the mood before you showed any interest? I promise you, there were lots of times when she wasn't. But women have learned a lot about how to turn themselves on—to throw that switch, as you call it. I don't see why men can't learn to do that too."

"You know," he said, and it was impossible to doubt his sincerity, "I absolutely never thought of that."

"I don't mean perfectly or every time," I explained, "but often enough to have more reciprocity between you."

His wife Donna asked, "Does this feel like a new responsibility you've been handed?"

"Hell no!" her husband exclaimed. "It feels like I've just been told about a power I never knew I had!" The issue of self-responsibility shows up in many more contexts than we ordinarily suspect.

I am responsible for the congruence or lack of congruence between my statement that I love you and my behavior toward you. No one can act lovingly all the time. But successful relationships (meaning relationships that yield a high measure of satisfaction and fulfillment to both parties) are those in which most of the time the partners hold to the context of love in their dealings with each other. Their actions reflect their professed feelings. They do not allow themselves to be so swamped by daily concerns that their dealings with each other become mechanical, spiritless, and detached. What is involved here is actually a kind of integrity, by which I mean congruence (or *integration*) between professed values and actual behavior.

If we are in a serious relationship and I say I love you, you have a right to expect that I will be interested in your thoughts and feelings, and that when you speak I will give you a respectful and attentive hearing. If I say I love you, you have a right to interpret this to mean that I will treat you kindly and benevolently. If I say I love you, you have a right to anticipate that I will be an emotional support system for you in times of stress or distress. If I say I love you, I am not promising never to be angry at you or disapproving of some aspect of your behavior, but I am promising to be your best friend, to be on your side, to give you empathy and compassion. If I say I love you, I am certainly declaring that your feelings and needs are important to me.

Granted, immature people who use the word "love" all too easily and promiscuously do not think through what they are committing themselves to when they make a declaration of romantic love. But self-responsible men and women do.

Sometimes the happiest of couples may fight; sometimes they may feel alienated. Sometimes our partner may do something that hurts or exasperates us. Sometimes we or our partner want passionately to be alone for a while. None of this is unusual or abnormal. None of this is a threat to romantic love or incompatible with the point I am making here.

One of the characteristics of mature, responsible love is the ability to know that we can love our partner deeply and nonetheless know times of feeling angry, irritated, or alienated, and that the truth and value of our relationship is not to be judged by moment-to-moment or day-to-day fluctuations in feeling. In healthy relationships there is an equanimity born of the knowledge that we have a history with our partner, we have a context, and we do not drop that context under the pressure of immediate hurts or disappointments. We remember. We retain the ability to see the whole picture. We do not reduce our partner to his or her last bit of behavior and define him or her solely by means of it.

To hold to this perspective is one of the challenges of romantic love, and the more mature and self-responsible we are, the more likely we are to meet it appropriately. We need the ability to remain in contact with the essence of our relationship in the face of temporary mishaps, conflicts, hurts, or estrangement. We need the ability to see the essence of our partner beyond what our partner may be doing at this moment. We need not to step outside the moment but to see the essence of our relationship and our partner *in* the moment, even when the moment is not a happy one.

But the more dependent we are, the less individuated and resourceful, the harder it is to hold to this perspective. If, unconsciously, we see our partner primarily as our caretaker; as someone who exists to make the world right for us; someone whose purpose is to satisfy our needs; someone to give us safety, security, and happiness, then we feel betrayed and resentful any time he or she does not fulfill that role. This is why I have always said that romantic love is for grown-ups.

I am responsible for carrying my own weight in the relationship. This point is an amplification of the preceding paragraph.

Throughout this book I have stressed that autonomy and self-responsibility are the natural condition of a successfully evolved adult, but that it is a state too many men and women fail to reach. Their bodies have matured more than their minds. Psychologically, they retain the orientation of someone much younger than their actual years.

"Maturity" and "immaturity" describe success or failure in an individual's biological, intellectual, and psychological evolution to an adult stage of development. With regard to intimate relationships, certain aspects of maturity are especially important:

- The development of genuine self-esteem.

- The development of autonomy. With a capacity for self-reliance we are able to face our partner as an independent equal. We do not look to another person to create our self-esteem, or make us happy, or fill the void of an otherwise meaningless life.

- The development of our own set of values so that we know what is important to us and what we care about, what is dispensable and what is indispensable. We can select a partner with some degree of realism.

- The development of internal resources so that we are not bowled over by the normal difficulties, obstacles, and frictions of life in general and of a relationship in particular. We can respond to challenges with confidence, optimism, and determination.

When men and women do not attain psychological adulthood, the danger is that unconsciously they expect others to assume responsibility for their existence, especially for their emotional life. They may be perfectly willing to earn their own living; that is not the focus here. But they wait for others to make them happy. They imagine that the right person can provide them with feelings of self-worth, can spare them the necessity of independence, can help them avoid the fact of their ultimate aloneness. And as we have already said, they typically feel hurt, resentful, and depressed when others fail to live up to their expectations.

Many men and women carry into adulthood so much unfinished business from childhood and so many unresolved conflicts that they enter the arena of intimate relationships with terrible handicaps. Blind to their own incapacities, they count on love to perform a miracle. When the miracle does not happen, they blame love. Or they blame their partner.

"I can't understand how any grown-up person can talk seriously about romantic love," said an embittered divorcée of thirty-five still trapped in the problems of a four-year-old girl. All her life she had been vainly trying to win affection from a cold, unresponsive father. She was shocked and disappointed when soon after marriage she realized that her husband too had emotional needs. She had imagined that she had to be aware only of her own. "Anyway," she added, "men don't know how to love."

Non-autonomous men and women may organize their whole life around the desire to please and to be taken care of, or, alternatively, to control, dominate, manipulate, and even command the satisfaction of their needs and wants. They tend not to trust the authenticity of anyone's caring and loving. They never feel that they are enough.

Whether they act out helplessness and dependence, or are controlling, overprotective, responsible, or grown-up, there is an underlying sense of inadequacy, of nameless deficiency that they feel only other human beings can remedy. Whether they seek completion and fulfillment through domination or submission, through controlling or being controlled, through ordering or obeying, there is the same sense of emptiness, a void in the center of their being, a hole where an autonomous self failed to develop. They have not learned to transfer the source of their approval from others to self. They have not learned self-responsibility.

Often two such persons marry with the tacit agreement that one will play child and one will play parent. Neither is comfortable relating adult to adult. It is as if one had said to the other, "I will be helpless, needy, dependent, a taker rather than a giver, and in exchange you can enjoy feeling superior." It is as if the other had said, "I will play the strong, supportive, parent figure, the one who carries the burdens for both of us, the martyr at times, and you can enjoy feeling safe and give me unconditional adoration." Inside the one who plays the child role is a disowned adult who will sooner or later cry out for expression. Inside the one who plays the parent role is a disowned child who will sometimes cry out over unmet needs. Conflicts are inevitable. The one playing helpless will protest,

"Stop treating me like an infant!" And the one playing a tower of strength will protest, "Why should all the burdens be mine? Can't you hold up your own end of things?"

There are females who feel comfortable as a mother or as a child but not as a woman. There are males who feel comfortable as a father or as a child but not as a man. And they have a genius for finding each other. Then they can conspire to create their own kind of tormented nursery, calling it a marriage or a relationship.

Psychologists often explain the failure of a relationship in terms of a couple's unrealistic expectations. Unrealistic expectations can result in disaster, undeniably. But we need not abandon the ideal of romantic love as unrealistic if we recognize that it is an adventure for adults, not for children. It demands realism.

To be an adult does not mean abandoning the child part of our personality but integrating it as we grow in self-responsibility and autonomy. Without contradicting what I have said here, we can recognize that there is a child in each of us as part of our psyche, and that the child is to be accepted, loved, and appreciated, not denied, disowned, or repudiated.* Mature men and women can love and enjoy the child in their partner, can delight in sometimes nurturing the child, *because the child is not all there is.* The child is part of the adult they love.

To nurture is to love not only our partner's strength but also his or her fragility, not only what is powerful in our partner but also what is delicate, not only what is grown-up but also what is young. In no sense, however, does this mean encouraging behavior that is destructive to our partner or to ourselves. It does not mean putting up with everything at the expense of our own well-being. It does not mean surrendering our judgment or our sanity. But it does mean giving support when possible and appropriate.

---

*I discuss this issue in *How to Raise Your Self-Esteem.*

There are moments when all of us want temporarily to abandon the responsibilities of adulthood, want to be stroked, pampered, cared for almost as a child, and there is no implication of immaturity in this. It is merely part of being human, merely the need for a special form of rest. When our partner gives us this nurturing, we feel loved. Giving it to our partner is one of the ways we express love. But such moments are significant because they are exceptions, not the basic pattern of our existence.

I am responsible for my happiness in the relationship. In light of what I have already said about happiness, this point can be made very briefly. If I carry the flame of happiness within me, and if I accept primary responsibility for keeping that flame alive, there is no question but that a fulfilling romantic relationship can greatly enhance my joy. We often hear people in love say, "He (she) makes me so happy." We may like giving our partner the credit. But it is not a statement to be taken literally. It would be more accurate to say, "My partner contributes so much joy to my life."

None of us can sustain happiness in another if that other feels essentially dependent on us for emotional well-being. The person may be contented or even joyful for a while at the start of our love affair, but eventually depression or sadness will resurface, if that is the basic theme of the personality. I can share my happiness with you, and we can enhance each other's happiness, just as we can share and enhance each other's excitement with life, but we cannot create joy in a space where before us there was only uncontested pain.

And consider what a burden it would be if our partner confronted us daily with the unspoken (or even spoken!) message "Make me happy—that's your role in our relationship." Could romantic love survive?

Learning Self-Responsibility in Relationships

The interesting thing is that I have rarely encountered a client, no matter how immature, who did not at some level understand what self-responsibility in an intimate relationship means. If the knowledge is not explicit, it is implicit.

I learned this principally through sentence-completion work. Over the years I gave clients a stem such as "If I operated five percent more self-responsibly in my marriage [or relationship]—." I consistently received endings such as:

> I wouldn't always blame my partner for my unhappiness.
>
> I'd be more empathetic.
>
> I wouldn't allow myself to blow up so often over trivia.
>
> I would give to my partner what I want my partner to give to me.
>
> I'd be kinder.
>
> I'd be more honest about my dissatisfactions.
>
> I'd take more responsibility for my emotions.
>
> I'd keep my promises better.
>
> I'd be fairer.
>
> I wouldn't get into self-pity so much.
>
> We could relate as equals.
>
> We could give each other respect.

Occasionally a client makes the error of thinking that self-responsibility means taking care of all our needs ourselves. We have already observed that we should not confuse self-responsibility with some false notion of absolute self-sufficiency. There are clearly many respects in which we need each other. If I deny and disown the ways in which I need you, I will almost certainly be blind to the ways in which you need me and I will fail you, no matter how much I may love you. If I am oblivious to my own need for nurturing, as men in particular often are, I am unlikely to be sensitive to yours. Empathy for another has its roots in self-awareness. This truth, so obvious to me now, is one I had to learn personally over some years, and I cannot claim that I was a quick student.

Most people do not need to heal all the wounds of childhood before learning to operate more self-responsibly in intimate relationships. In therapy we operationalize the idea of self-responsibility—translate it into specific behaviors—and coach people to learn and implement appropriate skills. What is most important, however, is the first step: the *idea* of self-responsibility. This is understanding and setting the goal of living and relating in a new way.

I realize that no one exists merely to serve me; that I must be prepared to give what I hope to receive; that grown-up relationships are reciprocal, not unilateral; and that if we do not do what is in our power to support the vitality of the relationship, we are implicitly counting on our partner to make up the deficit.

It is easier to dismiss romantic love as adolescent foolishness or to curse life as malevolent than to embrace what romantic love asks of us and hold ourselves accountable.

7

Accountability in Organizations

Most of us who work for a living do so in organizations of one kind or another. Let us therefore carry our examination of self-responsibility into this realm by considering what the concept means and how it can be inspired in contexts where people work together toward shared goals.

Recently I was asked by a firm that employed about two thousand people to work with "the lower one thousand" in creating an organizational culture of high accountability. I said I would need to begin not with the lower one thousand but with roughly the hundred most senior executives, explaining that if I could not enroll them in the project, if I could not win their enthusiasm and support, there was no way to make the undertaking successful. The CEO declined; he did not wish to become involved; he saw it as a problem of "the troops." That alone told me why his company was having problems. In any organization, personal responsibility and accountability—and culture change—begin at the top.

A modern business organization is a major transmitter of

values. The principles by which it operates and the way it treats its employees, suppliers, and customers radiate out through the world like radio waves. Today, a business is more than a place to produce goods or services. It is a social club, a community, a school, and perhaps even, as a source of learned values, a church. It is an environment that can have a profound impact on souls.

No one can remain unaffected by how he or she is treated eight hours a day, five days week—nor by the ethical behavior witnessed in associates and superiors. A company whose leaders and managers exhibit a high level of personal integrity, responsibility, and respect for the individual exert one kind of influence; a company whose leaders and managers exhibit the opposite exert a different kind of influence. But both kinds have an impact—immediately on their organization and, ultimately, on the culture at large.

A few leaders and managers understand the nature of their responsibility as role models and value setters. My impression is that the majority do not. They do not realize how closely they are watched, how the smallest details of their speech and behavior are noted; they do not know what an influence they have. They do not understand how organizational cultures are formed, let alone how their influence spreads beyond the borders of their own company.

What is becoming clearer, however, is what organizations need if they are to be competitive in a rapidly changing global economy—an economy in which the chief source of wealth is not land, machinery, or capital but ideas, information, *minds*. Whatever the merits of total quality management, reengineering, right-sizing, or any other such currently fashionable programs—and their merits are not in contention—the ultimate challenge to every business organization today is how to inspire the workforce to give its best: to be innovative, committed to continuous improvement, *and accountable.*

"How," business leaders wonder, "do we get our people to

take individual responsibility for the success of our company? How do we create a culture of personal accountability?"

The urgency of these questions arises from the extraordinary development in business in the past few decades. We have moved from a manufacturing economy to an information economy. Scientific and technological breakthroughs have been happening faster and faster. The rate of change has inevitably accelerated and continues to accelerate. The old command-and-control style of management has given way to one that actively seeks the intellectual contribution of everyone participating in production at all levels of an organization. The days are gone when businesses were run by a few people at the top who possessed all the knowledge relevant to their enterprise and did all of the thinking while everyone "below" merely carried out instructions. Now, with the advent of computers, knowledge is spread rapidly throughout the organization and everyone is expected to take responsibility for contributing ideas that can advance the goals of the company. Employees are expected to be capable of self-management and independent thinking. When they see problems or difficulties, they are expected to initiate the search for solutions. Obedience is no longer the great virtue it was once held to be; it has been replaced by the demand for innovativeness and responsibility. The challenge is: How can organizations inspire these behaviors?

To the extent that they are able to answer this challenge successfully, they gain enormous competitive advantage in the marketplace—and they contribute to the spread of self-responsibility in our society.

A note before proceeding: Very little in this chapter is not readily transferable from organizations to marriage, child-rearing, and family life in general. I hope that readers whose interest may not extend to the world of business will nonetheless find in this discussion ideas they can usefully apply in nonbusiness domains.

Creating a Context for Self-Responsibility

When I speak of leaders in this discussion, I do not mean only the CEO of an organization: I mean anyone, from CEO to manager to team facilitator to supervisor, who takes responsibility for conveying a vision, purpose, or task and for inspiring others to work toward its realization. In a particular situation anyone can be a leader who is willing to take on what it entails. If, for example, a group is floundering and one person says, "Here is what needs to be done"—that person at that moment may become a leader.

If a leader is to inspire self-responsibility in others, he or she must be perceived to practice it. This means:

- Being proactive rather than reactive

- Manifesting a high level of consciousness, focus, and purpose

- Taking responsibility for every choice, decision, and action without blaming or finding alibis

- Being fully accountable for all promises and commitments made

- Being clear on what is and is not within his or her power

- Being task-focused rather than focused on self-aggrandizement

- Being results-focused rather than turf-protecting

- Being able to bounce back from defeat, setbacks, or adversity and continue moving toward goals, rather than surrendering to despair

- Demonstrating an unmistakable commitment to facing reality, whether pleasant or unpleasant

On this last, the extraordinary transformation of General Electric under the leadership of CEO Jack Welch clearly relates to the values he modeled and strove to inspire in his people—in his own words, "self-confidence, candor, and *an unflinching willingness to face reality, even when it's painful* [italics added]."

When these traits are present in the CEO and other leaders in an organization, the result is much the same as when they are modeled by parents in a family: A context is established in which it is most likely that these traits will be absorbed and exhibited by others. The conclusion is drawn: *This is how human beings are to act; this is the norm here; this is what is expected of me.*

But there is more to the process of creating an organizational culture of accountability than appropriate modeling. Leaders have to think through the policies that will inspire the desired mind-set among employees. For example:

Require clarity concerning what is expected. This means that leaders must be absolutely clear, and see to it that the relevant persons are absolutely clear, about what each individual in an organization is accountable for. Some years ago the CEO of a medium-sized business gave me the assignment of finding out why there was not a higher level of accountability in his firm and what could be done about it. I suggested that we begin by asking each of his senior managers to write a memo stating what precisely they understood themselves to be responsible for and also what they *would like* to be responsible for. What surfaced immediately was tremendous confusion. In some instances, two or more executives held themselves exclusively responsible for the same aspect of the business; but for other aspects, *no one* thought he or she was responsible. In other words, some areas were given too much attention, which led to one kind of problem, while other areas were neglected, which led to another kind of problem. The next step was to review, redefine, and gain agreement concerning each person's area of accountability. This process was repeated with all the people who reported to each of these managers. The same kind of memo was requested, the same kind of confusion was uncovered, and the same remedial action was taken. Until each person knew what was expected of him or her, there could be no question of appropriate accountability.

Seek information regarding people's work goals. When you ask people what they *would like* to be accountable for, you can sometimes elicit useful information about their aspirations and ambitions. The best people in any organization are always looking to move beyond their job descriptions and, whenever possible, this is an attitude to be nurtured and supported. Give people all the responsibilities they can reasonably handle. Ask more of them and support them in asking more of themselves. When possible, assign tasks and projects slightly beyond the individual's known capabilities.

Be task-centered, not ego-centered. When we keep our encounters focused on reality and the objective needs of the situation, we support a climate of self-responsibility rather than permitting a dispute to deteriorate into a conflict of personalities. The focus should be "What are the facts? What needs to be done?" and *not* "Whose wishes will prevail—yours or mine?" The individual should ask, "What are my *reasons for taking this position?*" and not, "What is my rank in the organization?"

Invite feedback on the kind of boss/leader/manager you are. Let your people see that you are honestly interested in the image you project and how you affect others. Let them know you understand the principle that "you are the kind of manager your people say you are." Let them know, also, that if they have a grievance against you, you expect them to communicate it as quickly as possible—and set an example of open, nondefensive listening. Convey that you have little tolerance for grievances that are never expressed but that fester privately into bitterness and resentment. Exemplify self-responsibility in this area and make it clear that you require it of others.

Give corrective feedback without blaming. If someone's behavior is unacceptable, describe it, point out its consequences, including how other people are affected, and spell out the kind of behavior you require instead. Stay focused on fact and avoid character assassination. Communicate the belief that your listener *would want to know* if his or her behavior is undesirable, troublesome, or offensive. By keeping the focus on reality and avoiding put-downs or personal attacks, you speak to the self-responsible adult in the other party and discourage an evasive or defensive response.

Help people to experience themselves as the source of their actions and tune them into the why. If someone does superior work or makes an excellent decision, do not limit yourself to praise, but invite him or her to explore how and why it happened. Help the person by asking appropriate questions, to identify what made the achievement possible. For example, what was the mental process behind it? As a result, the person doesn't write off the achievement to "luck" but experiences him- or herself as the responsible causal agent, and you thereby increase the likelihood of such behavior being repeated. By the same logic, if someone does unacceptable work or makes a bad decision, practice the same principle. Do not limit yourself to corrective feedback, but invite an exploration of what caused the error, again stressing responsibility and minimizing the chance of a repetition.

Establish clear and unequivocal performance standards. This is one aspect of the wider issue of communicating people's responsibilities. Employees need to know a leader's/manager's/boss's nonnegotiable expectations regarding the quality of work. They need to know that this is the *minimum* expected of them. Non-accountability at this level is completely unacceptable.

Let problems stay with the person who created them. When someone's behavior creates a problem, ask him or her to provide a solution, if possible. Try to avoid handing down ready-made solutions that spare the person from taking a new initiative or developing new ideas. Say "Now that we agree on the nature of the problem, what to do you propose do about it?" Do not deny people the experience of learning from their struggle with this question.

Focus on finding solutions, not blaming. When things go wrong, the question should not be, Whose fault is it?, but What needs to be done? Convey in every way possible that blaming is an irrelevant distraction. The name of the game is *results,* not accusations. Ask "What are your ideas on how this situation can be improved or corrected?"

Give people the resources for self-responsibility. People cannot be accountable for what you have asked them to do if they are not given the appropriate resources, information, and authority. Remember that there is no responsibility without power. It is demoralizing to give people the first but not the second. An occasional hero will rise above circumstances and assert a power that no one has given him or her, taking responsibility and exercising ingenuity and initiative far beyond the call of duty. But it is unfair and unreasonable of management to count on that.

Remember what your job is. A great leader is not someone who comes up with brilliant solutions but rather one who inspires his or her people to come up with brilliant solutions. Like a great coach, a great parent, or a great psychotherapist, a great leader/manager *draws out* the best in people but does not do their work for them. Sometimes this means controlling their own exhibitionistic impulses or desire to be admired.

Work at changing aspects of the organizational culture that thwart or frustrate self-responsibility. Sometimes outmoded procedures carried over from the command-and-control management model frustrate the self-responsibility that you are promoting. For example, when significant decision making must be passed up the chain of command, those close to the decision are disempowered and paralyzed. Such policies stifle innovation and creativity, and make personal accountability all but impossible.

Avoid micromanaging. Micromanaging is the enemy of autonomy and self-responsibility. If you want people to operate self-responsibly, avoid overdirecting, overobserving, overreporting, and overmanaging. Let people know what needs to be done *and leave them alone.* Let people struggle. Let them take the initiative in asking for help if and when they need it, but do not take the decision out of their hands. Just as parents who overmanage a young person can obstruct evolution to adulthood, so leaders who micromanage inhibit the very traits they need most for the success of their enterprise. Young people learn self-responsibility in part by being *trusted;* so do men and women in an organization. When a leader conveys belief in people's competence and worth, people are far more likely to rise to the occasion. Do not step in *unless it is absolutely necessary.*

Plan and budget for innovation. It is unreasonable to ask for self-responsibility, initiative, innovation, and creativity and then announce that there are no resources to support and implement the contributions people make. The predictable result is that people will fall into (relative) passivity and demoralization. Organizations need to make self-responsibility *practical.*

Find out what people want and need to perform optimally, and provide it. The less people feel in control of their work, the more they are dispirited, unambitious, unempowered, and unable to self-generate. One of the most useful questions to ask people is, "What do you need to feel more in control of your work?" If possible, give it to them. If what you want from them is excitement, autonomy, and a personal stake in the success of your company, try to give them what they need to achieve these things.

Reward self-responsible behavior. Reward self-assertiveness, intelligent risk taking, acts of initiative, unsolicited problem solving, and a strong orientation toward action. Too many companies pay lip service to these values but in practice reward those who conform, don't ask difficult questions, don't challenge the status quo, and remain essentially passive while going through the motions of their job description. If you want to create a culture of innovation and responsibility, look for opportunities to reward and celebrate it. Let your responses signal *That is what we want.* When people do things right in important or original ways, broadcast their stories through your entire organization. No aspect of an organization's culture is more revealing than the kind of stories that circulate.

Thus far, we have discussed the general principles for creating a culture of responsibility and accountability. Now, to clarify the kind of coaching that may be required, we will examine some common ways that people fail to show these traits.

Avoiding Self-Responsibility

Among the many ways that people avoid self-responsibility is by failing or refusing to see what they see and know what they know.

A while ago I was having lunch with a friend who complained about a recently acquired assistant. He had long struggled to obtain permission to hire an assistant and now he was in despair about his choice. "She's great at the conceptual level," my friend said, "but when it comes to the daily nuts-and-bolts of being organized and handling details competently and reliably, she's a calamity. Here's a typical example of the kind of thing she does. I ask her to photocopy an article and send it to a client. She does it all right, but what the client receives, stapled, is not pages 1-2-3-4-5 but rather 1-4-2-5-3. Afterwards, of course, she's always apologetic, but she does things like that almost every day. I've tried everything I know to improve her performance and nothing works. I'm reluctant to fire her and begin the search all over again, but it's driving me crazy."

Then, later in the lunch, after we had talked about other things, he began talking about his assistant again. "I'm thinking about what you teach about self-responsibility. I'm wondering if I'm in any way at fault for getting into this mess." We sat silently for a couple of minutes while he reflected. Then he turned to me and declared, "I think I've got it. When I interviewed her, her credentials and references were excellent, and I was dying to make a decision because I'd already interviewed a lot of people. I hated the process, and I wanted to be done with it. Toward the end I asked her, 'How are you on being well organized and on handling details?' She answered, 'I try to be good . . . but things happen.' That should have tipped me off. *'Things happen.'* That was the moment to thank her and let her go. Instead, because I was impatient, because I wanted to get back to business, I didn't stay focused on what I was hearing and what it meant. I didn't let her statement fully register. Now it's come back to haunt me. She was telling me that she didn't take responsibility for seeing that things got done right and I chose not to hear her. Now I'm paying for my unconsciousness."

In our business life (and of course in our personal life), one of the ways we avoid responsibility is by pretending ignorance or unawareness. Talking to a prospective employee, partner, customer, client, supplier, or lover, we tune out or selectively inattend to information that would be disturbing. Then, when disappointment or disaster strikes, we are able to cry, "But how could I have known?" and to persuade ourselves that we are victims of unforeseeable misfortune.

On many occasions I have counseled people with a propensity for getting into bad deals with people who betrayed them. Almost always we could find warning signs along the way that were ignored at a conscious level. By pretending not to see and not to know, they could play out the drama of their "victimhood" while disclaiming all responsibility for their plight.

During the past two decades, any number of business concerns have failed or lost major market share because leaders chose to ignore clear economic markers that strategies that had once been adaptive were not responsive to new realities. What their more successful competitors chose to see and know, these leaders chose not to see or know. What followed was often an orgy of alibis and blame that did nothing to redeem their company. When things began to go wrong, these executives could have asked themselves, *What am I pretending not to know?* Of course, this requires ruthless honesty, but without it, self-responsibility is impossible.

Another way of avoiding responsibility, like ignoring, evading, or denying troublesome realities, is to *manufacture confusion.* "No one told me what to do." "I didn't realize there was a hurry for this." "My supervisor told me to do it one way, and you told me to do it another. How was I supposed to know what to do? I didn't know, so I did nothing." "The instructions were ambiguous." "No one came to check up on me, so how could I know if I was doing it right?"

When people operate self-responsibly, when they make a commitment to deliver a certain result and hold themselves accountable, *they do not allow confusion to remain.* They do whatever is needed to clear up the confusion. Their goal is not to avoid blame but to deliver what was promised, *whatever it takes.* This is accountability in action.

Another way of avoiding responsibility is by taking too narrow a view of what you are accountable for: the strategy of "But this is not my job!" Passive employees look at problems in their company, see mistakes being made—for example, a defective part rolling off the line—or hear a recurring customer complaint. But since addressing such issues is not in their job description, they sit idly by, watching problems mount up, never bothering even to sound a warning, let alone take responsibility for a solution.

A client of mine, an executive in a firm that made industrial tools, began complaining one day about the inefficiency of one of his company's suppliers. "If we don't get delivery of the units when promised, we can't keep our own delivery commitments. We're supposed to send off a very important order next week, and one of the components that should have arrived a month ago still hasn't arrived! No one seems to be doing anything about it in the supply firm or in our own!"

"And what are *you* doing about it?" I inquired.

He look astonished and replied, "Oh, I just happen to know about it, but it's not my problem, not my department, not my job."

I asked him as a thought experiment to imagine what he *might* do with the premise that the success of the firm where he worked was his personal responsibility, insofar as he had the power to act.

He brightened and said, "Oh, there's plenty I could do," and proceeded to tell me what. I gave him a homework assignment: Every morning for the next two weeks to write six to ten endings for the stem "If I operate five percent more self-responsibly in the office today—."

Yet another way of avoiding responsibility is by looking at a festering problem and telling yourself, "Wait and see." In other words, "Sooner or later someone will do something."

The CEO of a company that manufactured women's clothing knew that his two most senior executives were locked in an adversarial, competitive relationship to which the best interests of the firm were often subordinated. He was a man who disliked confrontations of any kind, however, and the thought of confronting these two men with the reality of what they were doing was very uncomfortable. He ignored the harm they were doing to the business and told himself that "Eventually they'll come to their senses." When the situation deteriorated still more and he sat passively by, the board of directors replaced him. He was devastated. "I gave my best to that company," he said to his friends. "I feel like a total victim."

One easily recognizable way to evade responsibility is by blaming. "It's not my fault, it's X's fault." In a troubled organization, nothing is more common than for one department or group to blame another for any setback or misfortune. As Conners, Smith, and Hickman observe in *The Oz Principle:*

> . . . marketing blames R&D for designing products or features the customer doesn't need instead of the ones marketing knows the customer wants; sales attacks marketing for such inadequate support as ill-conceived brochures or mistargeted commercials; manufacturing accuses sales of signing off on poor forecasts that cause either too many back orders or too much inventory; R&D points the finger at manufacturing for not resolving manufacturability problems on the factory floor; vice presidents heap scorn on directors for not taking more responsibility, while directors chide vice presidents for either not providing sufficient guidelines or not letting go. Around and around it goes, a merry-go-round of accusations that does nothing to solve an organization's problems.

Blaming has a long tradition. In the Garden of Eden, Adam blamed Eve for eating the apple, Eve blamed the serpent for enticing her, and the serpent probably said, "I couldn't help it—it's my nature. Blame it on my nature."

Parents see this behavior all the time with children. "I didn't do it—Johnny did it!" We associate growing up with relinquishing responses of this kind.

The problem is that when we are blaming, we are not examining our contribution to the problem and we are also not looking for solutions. Blaming is a barrier between us and a correction of the situation.

When people are more concerned with covering themselves and establishing that whatever happened isn't their fault, self-esteem suffers, learning suffers, growth suffers, and of course the business suffers.

As a last example of ways in which we can avoid appropriate self-responsibility, we look at a subtler form of passivity in the attitude that "I have done enough." In this instance, we do not judge our accountability by whether we have reached the goal to which we had committed but by whether we have made an effort. We go through the motions to get a problem solved or a goal achieved; then we tell ourselves, "I have done enough. No one can legitimately blame me. I have tried." We do not ask, "What *else* can I do? (And what *else* can I do? And what *else* can I do?)" But the people who persist in asking this question are the ones who carry the world.

Self-responsibility and accountability are not omnipotent. There will be times when, despite all the dedication and perseverance in the world, we will still fail to achieve our goal. No guilt or self-reproach is needed. We can honestly say, "I have exhausted every solution I can think of." But many people in organizations (as well as in their private lives) fall far short of this point. They are much too quick to tell themselves, "I have done enough; no one can blame me"—as if to avoid blame were the goal of life.

Coaching for Self-Responsibility

The strategies for avoiding responsibility that we have just described may not be the only ones a leader or manager will encounter, but they are the most common. Operating in the role of coach, how might he or she respond?

When someone tells a tale of woe with the speaker cast in the role of victim, it is useful to explore with him or her the questions, "Was there anything you were choosing not to look at? Anything you were pretending not to see or know? Any early warning signs you ignored? Any questions you thought of asking, then brushed aside? Any issues you knew needed to be confronted but blanked out of your mind?" This ought to be done without reproaches or accusations, but as an exercise in self-examination and learning done with goodwill and an earnest desire to get at the facts.

The person may have to retell the story several times before areas of avoided awareness emerge. And they do not *always* emerge. Perhaps there was nothing he or she was refusing to look at. Just the same, the process of inquiry has value as a discipline. Looking at a business difficulty, setback, or defeat in this light is a way of keeping in the center of everyone's consciousness the theme of self-responsibility and accountability.

I like to work in this area using sentence completion. I might propose multiple endings for stems such as "If I had been willing to see what I saw and know what I knew—"; "One of the issues I might have ignored was—"; "One of the issues I might have paid more attention to was—"; "One of the issues I might have been reluctant to confront was—"; "Looking back now, it occurs to me that—." (Note the frequent use of the word "might." The purpose is to make the stem as gentle and nonthreatening as possible.)

When people explain themselves by "confusion," it is useful to inquire, "What could you have done to resolve your confusion? What actions could you have taken to obtain greater clarity? What might be the benefits of allowing yourself to remain confused? Can you imagine anyone in your situation acting differently from the way you did? What options didn't you exercise?" Such questions are meant to be respectful and not adversarial. The purpose is to expand consciousness and, as a consequence, improve performance.

We go over the person's story, point by point and moment by moment, until it becomes clear when and how he or she might have resolved the confusion. What we are really teaching is a method of self-examination. The goal is to make it second nature so that a higher level of self-management has been attained and further counseling on this issue becomes unnecessary.

When dealing with the "but it's not my job!" mentality, we need to explain, first of all, that in a modern organization a job description is a statement of the *minimum* expected of an employee. If the employee has any serious career aspirations, he or she needs to know that winners do not limit themselves to the formalities of their job description but are always on the lookout for ways to expand the range of their learning and their contribution to the organization. Modern organizations have less and less use for people whose idea of a job is to go through a set of motions from nine to five with zero independent thinking and zero personal initiative. That mentality might have been acceptable on an assembly line in 1910, but it is utterly obsolete today. These messages need to be conveyed, however, not merely by a coach in response to an individual problem but by the entire organizational culture, using executive talks, company newsletters, celebrations of unusual "beyond-the-call-of-duty" contributions, performance reviews, and the reward system. People need to be signaled daily that they are expected to think and to show initiative. If a colleague drops the ball, their responsibility is not to watch passively but *to pick it up.*

If you have the misfortune to be working for a company that

does not understand and appreciate this kind of self-responsibility, it may be time to look for a new job—unless, as sometimes happens, you are willing to take on the challenge of changing their organizational culture and see some possibility of success. In general, however, this discussion is directed to firms that *value* self-responsibility in their people.

As for men and women who watch problems grow while doing nothing about it according to the "wait and see" policy, a coach might find it useful to explore such questions as, "What did you imagine would happen if you continued to do nothing about the problem? How did you fantasize it would get resolved? Who did you think was going to solve it? What did you tell yourself when you saw that no one was doing anything and the problem was worsening? How did you see your own responsibility in the matter? Were you behaving as you would want an employee to behave if you owned the company? What would you have wanted an employee to do that you were not doing? Under what circumstances, if any, can you imagine yourself taking more initiative in such situations?"

When I address such behavior, I often assign a week or two of writing six to ten endings every day for such incomplete sentences as "When I watch a growing problem and do nothing—"; "If I typically wait for other people to solve problems—"; "If I keep telling myself 'Someone (else) will do something'—"; "When I do nothing and the problem gets worse, I tell myself—"; "If I operate five percent more responsibly in the face of problems—"; "If I fully accept that no one is coming to rescue the situation—"; "I am becoming aware—"; "If I want to translate these learnings into action, I will need to—."

After the person completes this assignment, it is useful to discuss the endings and explore the new behaviors that are indicated. A month or two later, the person might be asked to write a self-evaluation.

The *blaming* orientation is often a challenge to coaches because it can be deeply entrenched in a person's psyche—a response learned long ago in childhood and never really outgrown. And even when it is not deep in the person's psychology, it can still be difficult to cope with because the blaming may to some extent be justified (which does *not* mean that blaming is a productive response).

Directors may be *right* in some of their grievances against management, R&D may be *right* in some of its complaints about marketing. That is not the point. What we want to substitute for a blaming attitude—justified or unjustified or somewhat justified—is an attitude of *what can I do to correct the situation?* We want to substitute proactivity for reactivity, and solution seeking for fault finding.

Refining this point still further, we need to ask, What in my circumstances can I change and what can I not change? If some changes are possible, what steps can I take to accomplish them? And, within the limits of what I cannot change, what avenues are open to achieve my goals and commitments? Now we are back to an earlier point: What can I do? And what *else* can I do? (And what *else* can I do? And what *else* can I do?) This is the only way to eliminate blaming.

It is difficult to get rid of undesirable behavior if we do not replace it with something else. We will not get rid of blaming by showing that it is counterproductive. We need to teach what to do instead.

It is often helpful to invite people to explore such questions as, "If I took full responsibility for solving this problem—regardless of who else might be at fault—what might I do? If I don't like some of my circumstances and are determined to change them, what options do I have and what actions are possible to me? If I have to work around impediments I cannot remove, how can I still achieve my goals?"

Recently I read a story in *The Oz Principle,* mentioned above, that beautifully illustrates the idea I am after here, as well as several other of the ideas I am propounding. A young, struggling computer company, founded in a garage, finally sold its first computer to a *Fortune* 500 company on the opposite coast. There was an enormous sense of celebration and family solidarity among the people involved in this venture, and even the truck driver, who worked for a separate, independent company, was caught up in the spirit of excitement as he prepared to carry the computer across the country in his eighteen-wheeler.

The driver understood the supreme importance of delivering the computer on time. But, when he had been driving for almost eight hours, he pulled into his first weigh station and learned that his load was five hundred pounds over the legal limit. He knew that getting the legal approvals to proceed, with all the paperwork this would entail, would make him late for the promised delivery. He did not fall back on the attitude that "there's nothing I can do. It's not my fault. It's the fault of the people back at the computer company who failed to take the weight factor into consideration. I'll call the company and ask for instructions." Instead, he took responsibility for solving the problem. He dismantled the truck's front and rear bumpers, removed the extra water containers, and hid them under some nearby brush, planning to collect them again on the return route. This brought his rig fifty pounds under the legal limit. He was passed through and drove on to deliver the computer on schedule.

Note that he did not resort to blaming, nor did he fall into "confusion" or "it's not part of my job description to cope with problems of this kind," or any other escape mechanism that would have left the problem unsolved. Instead, with nothing but his own mind to guide him, he looked for and found a solution. Such is the everyday heroism of people who live by the code of self-responsibility.

If I may interject a personal note, I do not know what other people think of when they hear the word "morality," but for myself I will say this: I think of the mind state of that truck driver. At every level of ability and in every field of endeavor, it is that way of facing challenges on which all our lives depend.

Finally, how can people be helped to move beyond the "I have done enough" mentality? How can people be made to understand that the name of the game is to achieve results, not just to be "beyond reproach." No one would have faulted that truck driver if he was late in delivering the computer. But that was not the point. The point was delivering the computer on time, and this was what the driver understood and took responsibility for.

So coaching here entails such questions as, "How do you see the responsibilities of your job? What do you think are the limits of your responsibility? How do you decide when you have done enough? What do you think should be your next step when you have done everything you normally do and the problem is still unsolved or the goal still unreached? How do you decide when to stop trying? How do you justify that decision? If you were the owner of the company, do you think you might want an employee to persevere longer and harder than you did? Can you imagine putting virtually no limits on your commitment until your goal was reached? And how would you feel about doing that?"

A point of clarification is necessary here. I am emphatically not arguing for the idea that a person working for an organization should be willing to subordinate every other value of his or her existence—health, family, recreation, and so forth—to that of achieving the goals of the organization. That policy could generate gross irresponsibility toward oneself. I am not an advocate of self-sacrifice. Rather, I am seeking to convey the idea that within rational limits (that do not produce wreckage in the rest of your life), you need to scrutinize carefully what you mean by "doing enough" if the goal to which you are committed has not yet been reached.

Even allowing for this clarification, there can be legitimate differences among people in how much of their time, energy, and life they are willing to give to the organization that employs them. Obviously the people who give the most are likely to rise the highest. But not everyone's desire is to rise as high as possible; not everyone is equally ambitious. Sooner or later I am always quoting my favorite Spanish proverb: "'Take what you want,' said God, 'and pay for it.'"

Having said all this, I will observe that there are people who maintain a decent private life apart from the job and take good care of themselves. At work, they are firmly committed to giving everything they have to achieve the goals they have agreed to and to respond appropriately to the situations that confront them. These are the people who understand accountability.

A final word on the subject of coaching. The effectiveness of the above recommendations presupposes an organization whose structure and incentive system *supports, facilitates, and rewards self-responsibility*. If it doesn't, if self-responsible behaviors are penalized or met with indifference, it is unreasonable to expect most people to exhibit high levels of self-responsibility. One day, when I was discussing this issue with Warren Bennis, head of the Leadership Institute at USC, he made an observation that goes to the heart of the matter: "About any behavior thought to be desirable by an organization, it's useful to ask: Is this behavior rewarded, punished, or ignored? The answer to this question tells you what an organization really cares about, not what it says it cares about."

Business and Society

When writing about the new world of business it is easy and misleading to imply that business organizations in general understand the extraordinary transformations that have taken place in the last few decades and that are still under way. The truth is, most business people are stuck in older ways of thinking about their work and wedded, to varying degrees, to the outmoded command-and-control style of management. The rhetoric about respect for the individual, the importance of everyone's contribution to production, and the value of independent initiative are far ahead of everyday business practice. Too many organizations still punish mistakes more than they reward success and still prize conformity above self-responsibility. Often initiative and self-responsibility are praised in theory and penalized in practice. The structures and incentive systems of such organizations do not support the behaviors most lauded in the abstract and most needed for success.* Naturally they pay a price for their errors in terms of loss of market share to more forward-looking competitors. Economic realities are pushing them in the direction they need to go. But some companies will be dragged into the twenty-first century kicking and screaming about the good old days, and some will not make it all, having become casualties of their own unconsciousness and fear of change. It is safe to say, however, that the trend is toward the kind of organizational culture I have been describing. The reason is that it alone is adaptive to a fast-moving, rapidly changing, ferociously competitive global economy.

So imagine if you will a future in which most people who work in organizations are educated in the ideals of self-responsibility and accountability. These values will find their way into our educational system because, sooner or later, what the marketplace requires, our school system provides. Parents will demand it: They want their children prepared for real life. This is one of the ways in which the wider culture is affected by the values that dominate the business community.

"Sometimes I feel like the leader not of a business but of a church or a temple," one CEO said to me. "I am so conscious that the values we uphold here go on reverberating far beyond our walls. It's an immense responsibility. To some extent, whatever people learn here, they take home with them. I want them to take home values we can all be proud of."

---

*For more on this subject, see my discussion of self-esteem in the workplace in *The Six Pillars of Self-Esteem.*

Each employee who is expected to practice self-responsibility and personal accountability on the job carries that idea out into the world at the end of the day. If it shapes behavior during working hours, it is likely to have an impact on the rest of his or her life. The probability is high that it will be transmitted to children and to other people with whom the employee interacts. That is the point this CEO was making.

The ideal of self-responsibility is not new. What is new is the extent to which business organizations require it of their people to remain competitive. In this lies hope for the future of our world.

8

A Culture of Accountability

Ultimately,
an attitude of self-responsibility must be generated from
within the individual. It cannot be "given" from the outside,
just as self-esteem cannot.

And yet we can appreciate that there are social environments in which people are more likely to learn self-responsibility and environments in which they are less likely. There are
social philosophies *and policies* that encourage independence,
and there are others that encourage dependence. The average
person is not so autonomous that he or she will generate the
appropriate attitudes in a culture that is rewarding the opposite.

So let us shift our examination of self-responsibility from
the "inside" to the "outside"—from the individual to the human environment in which he or she lives and acts.

I will begin with a story.

One of the pleasures in being a psychotherapist is the opportunity to experiment with mildly mischievous solutions to

clients' difficulties. Here is an incident taken from my clinical practice.

Nadine R. was a thirty-eight-year-old mother and office manager who worked on personal problems with me via the telephone. (I do a good deal of psychotherapy on the telephone with clients who call from other cities.) My office is in Los Angeles, and her home is in Minneapolis. This afternoon she sounded desperate.

"God, I wish you were a woman today!" were her first words. "I don't know if a man will have sympathy for this problem."

She presented the following dilemma. Her husband was a research scientist who had his own laboratory; she ran his office in addition to running their home and raising their two teenage boys. She made only one request of them: When she entered her kitchen to make dinner, she wanted to find the garbage pail empty and all dirty dishes in the dishwasher. Her husband and sons agreed to take turns discharging this responsibility but rarely followed through. Before she began to cook, she usually had to clean up the kitchen, which she resented. The men in her family agreed that she was absolutely right, only nothing ever changed.

"I've reasoned with them," Nadine said, "I've pleaded, I've screamed, I've begged—nothing works. I feel utterly ineffectual. What should I do?"

"Are you absolutely committed to getting a change?" I asked.

"I'd do *anything*," she declared.

"Good. I think you can help these gentlemen to keep their promises—if you'll do exactly as I say. We're going to conduct an experiment."

Next evening, when she found the kitchen dirty, she walked into the living room and began reading a book. When her puzzled husband and sons inquired about dinner, she answered, smiling pleasantly, "I don't cook in a dirty kitchen." (I had told her, "No reproaches and no explanations.") The men exchanged disoriented looks and disappeared into the kitchen. A few minutes later, when they informed her it was now spotless, she proceeded—cheerfully—to prepare their dinner.

The next night the kitchen was clean when she first entered it.

The night after that, the garbage pail was full again and there were dirty dishes on the counter. (I had told her this was likely.) Without saying a word, she went out and resumed her reading. Soon she heard them reproaching one another for not cleaning up and negotiating who would be responsible for what.

For several weeks, she entered a clean kitchen at dinnertime. I had warned her to be prepared for at least one more "test." But when once again she found the kitchen dirty, she was tempted to overlook it because of their recent efforts. They've been so *good,* she thought. I had cautioned her that this was the moment at which the experiment would succeed or fail, depending on the consistency of her response. So she summoned all her willpower and went back to her book.

That ended the problem. What she had not accomplished with years of words, she accomplished within weeks through her actions.

I said to her, "If something doesn't work, don't keep doing it. Pay attention to outcomes. You needed to change your behavior to get them to change theirs. You gave them a strong reason to cooperate with you and do what they had promised to do. The moral of the story is, When you hit a wall, look for new actions to take."

"What I finally saw," she remarked, "is that if I was always willing to make up for their defaults, I wasn't really giving them any persuasive reason to change. When I gave them a reality that required that they do what they had agreed to do—surprise, surprise—*their actions changed.*"

This story has implications for child-rearing and for society at large.

Encouraging Self-Responsibility in Young People

An attitude of self-responsibility is most likely to flourish where there is good, basic self-esteem. When parents and teachers convey their belief in a young person's competence and worth, they are laying the best possible groundwork not only for the emergence of self-esteem but also for self-responsibility and independence. What we want to discuss here are two simple ideas:

- Young people are most likely to learn self-responsibility from adults who personally exemplify it in their behavior.

- Young people are most likely to learn self-responsibility if their parents and teachers *require* it.

In other words, if adults *model* self-responsibility and convey their belief that young people are capable of operating self-responsibly *and are expected to do so*, and if adults deal with them consistently from this perspective, the probability is that young people will respond positively and grow into self-responsibility.

Children are unlikely to learn self-responsibility from adults who are passive, self-pitying, prone to blaming and alibis, and who invariably explain their life circumstances on the basis of someone else's actions or on "the system." Such adults do not teach self-responsibility, and if they do pay lip service to it, they are probably not convincing.

If, however, children grow up in a home or are educated in a school system among adults who hold themselves accountable for what they do, are honest about acknowledging their mistakes, carry their own weight in relationships, and work for what they want in life, there is a good probability, although never an absolute guarantee, that this behavior will be perceived as normal and as what is appropriate to a human being.

Occasionally, a child is so appalled by the passivity and immaturity of one or both parents that in reaction the child learns self-responsibility very early. But this is not the most likely outcome and in any event is a hard way to learn.

Apart from exemplifying self-responsibility themselves, the greatest contribution adults can make is to convey to young people that self-responsibility is what is expected and required. Here are examples of what this policy might mean in action:

- A boy makes so much noise at the dinner table that no else is able to enjoy the meal. Mother says, "You have a choice. You can eat by yourself in the kitchen, or you can hold the noise level down when we're eating. You decide." When the boy continues with his uproar, Mother says, "I see you've decided to eat by yourself"—and separates him from the family dinner table. Later, when he agrees to eat in a more acceptable manner, Mother says, "I'm glad you've decided to eat with us. We've missed you." She is helping her son to understand that he has choices and that actions have consequences, and that he is cared for. Note that she does so without lectures, insults, ridicule, or abuse; she speaks with respect for his dignity.

- A high school girl asks permission to use the family car. Permission is given on the understanding that she must always return the car with a full tank of gas; this is discussed explicitly between her and her father. Three times in a row she fails to fill the tank as promised. He withdraws driving privileges for a month, saying, "I see you've decided not to use the car for a while. I will respect your decision." When he overhears her telling a girlfriend, "My parents won't let me have the car 'cause I didn't deliver on my promise to bring it home with a full tank"—he later tells her, "Thank you for the honesty of your explanation to your friend. I appreciate your taking responsibility for your actions." This simple acknowledgment is worth more than any sermon on morality.

- A teenage boy who is hardworking and an A-student announces his intention to take a year off, after finishing high school, to travel. His father asks, "What are your plans for financing this adventure?" His son speaks of the money he has been saving and of the work he plans to do this coming summer to earn additional money. His father says, "I appreciate your strong sense of purpose. Tell you what I'll do—I'll match any amount of money you are able to get together by the time you're ready to go." He is not afraid to offer help to a boy who shows such self-motivation and independence.

- A daughter in her twenties, with a long record of acting irresponsibly and counting on her parents to bail her out, has been cautioned by her mother that she is now on her own and that her family may no longer be regarded as a financial resource. Just the same, the daughter phones and in a panicky voice announces that she has only two months' rent left and does not know what to do. "This is a real challenge for you," her mother says pleasantly. The daughter says, "My boss let me go just because I was late to work a few times last month." Her mother says, "Uh-huh." The daughter wails, "What will I do?" Her mother answers, "I really don't know." Disoriented because the old maneuvers aren't working, the daughter persists, "Soon I'll be out of money!" "This sounds like a real tough problem," her mother answers. "My boss is a real stinker," the daughter announces. Her mother inquires, "You mean, because he needed you at work on time?" *"Mother!"* the daughter shrieks, *"What am going to do?"* The mother responds benevolently, "I have absolute confidence in your ability to find a solution. I've been remiss in the past by bailing you out and not helping you develop your inner strength. Is there anything else, dear? I really need to be going now." The mother knows that by always rescuing her daughter in the past, she had given her grounds to believe she did not have to take responsibility for her own life. Now it is time to provide the education she regretted not providing years earlier. She knows that her daughter is not stupid and not infirm and is not going to die: She will find a way to survive and may become stronger in the process. Is success guaranteed? It cannot be. But in these circumstances her greatest gift to her daughter is to go "on strike." I have counseled many parents to this policy, and more often than not in later years their children acknowledged the wisdom of what was done. And I have seen children destroyed by parents who refused to stop being "helpful."

In nature, if we behave irresponsibly we suffer the consequences not because nature is "punishing" us but because of simple cause and effect. If we do not plant food, we do not reap a harvest. If we are careless about fire, we destroy our property. If we build a raft without securing the logs properly, the raft comes apart in the water and we may lose our belongings or drown. None of this happens because reality is angry with us. If reality could speak, it might say, "It's nothing personal."

Parents who wish to encourage self-responsibility teach consequences, teach cause and effect. We don't want to eat with you if you make the experience unpleasant for us. We won't lend you the car if you keep returning it with an empty tank. If you show evidence of self-responsibility, we'll be inspired to assist you in your goals. If we see you repeatedly living unthinkingly, we refuse to go on being a rescuer—we refuse to care more about your life than you do. *If you want dinner, honor your promise to keep the kitchen clean—I don't cook in a dirty kitchen.* In this way, we can teach natural consequences, not artificial punishments.

If other people are not willing to make up the deficit, no one would imagine he or she could get away with living irresponsibly. Reality would very quickly correct any such delusion. It is the intervention of others that allows some people to believe that theirs is to *wish* while it is the job of others to *provide,* theirs to *dream* while others must *act,* theirs to *suffer* while others must *produce solutions,* theirs to *feel* while others must *think.*

Unfortunately, we often see people working to make up for others' defaults, while wondering bitterly why those others aren't practicing self-responsibility. Yet are not those others daily given evidence that they can get away with their passivity and manipulative helplessness?

If there is one truth that psychologists of the most divergent views agree on, *it is that if you wish to encourage a particular pattern of behavior, you do not reward its opposite.*

This brings us to the subject of culture, political philosophy, and social policy.

Responsibility and Community

The traditional American values of individualism, self-reliance, self-discipline, and hard work had their roots, in part, in the fact that this country began as a frontier nation where everything had to be created.

To be sure, most Americans exhibited a strong sense of community, and they certainly practiced mutual aid. But this was not seen as a substitute for self-responsibility. Independent people helped one another when they could, but everyone was expected to carry his or her own weight. People were not encouraged to believe they enjoyed special "entitlements."

The Declaration of Independence proclaimed the revolutionary idea that a human being had a right to life, liberty, and the pursuit of happiness. This meant not that he or she was owed anything by others, but rather that others—including the government—were to respect the individual's freedom and the inviolability of his or her person. It is only by the use of force or fraud (which is an indirect form of force) that human rights can be infringed on, and it was force and fraud that were, in principle, barred from human relationships.

This rejection of the initiation of force in human relationships was the translation into political and social reality of the eighteenth-century precept of natural rights—that is, rights held by individuals not as a gift from the state but rather by virtue of being human. This idea was one of the great achievements of the Enlightenment.

The principle of inalienable rights was never adhered to with perfect consistency. The U.S. government claimed the privilege of certain exceptions from the very beginning. And yet the *principle* remained the guiding vision of the American system. For a very long time, it was what *America* stood for: Freedom. Individualism. Private property. The right to the pursuit of happiness. Self-ownership. The individual as an end in him- or herself, not a means to the ends of others, and not the property of family or church or state or society.

Lord Acton observed, "Liberty is not a means to a higher political end. It is itself the highest political end." This idea is what America was perceived to stand for and embody. The United States was the first country in the history of the world to be consciously created out of an idea—and the idea was liberty.

Observe that the inalienable rights on which this system was based were *negative* rights in that they were not claims on anyone else's energy or production. In effect, they merely proclaimed "Hands off!" They made no demands on others except to *abstain* from coercion. I may not impose my wishes or ideas on you by force, and you may not impose yours on me.

Human dealings are to be *voluntary*. We are to deal with one another by means of *persuasion*.

In the arena of political economy, the name given to this system in its purest, most consistent form was laissez-faire capitalism. But this is merely a synonym for freedom. *Capitalism is what happens when freedom of choice and action is recognized and protected by a government.*

In the nineteenth-century United States of America, with the development of a free-market society, people saw the sudden release of productive energy that had previously had no outlet. They saw life made possible for countless millions who had little chance for survival in precapitalist economies. They saw mortality rates fall and population growth rates explode upward. They saw machines—the machines that many of them had cursed, opposed, and tried to destroy—cut their workday in half while multiplying incalculably the value and reward of their effort. They saw themselves lifted to a standard of living no feudal baron could have conceived. With the rapid development of science, technology, and industry, they saw, for the first time in history, the liberated mind taking control of material existence.

In this country during the nineteenth century, productive activities were *predominantly* left free of government regulations, controls, and restrictions. True enough, there was always *some* government intervention into economic activities, and some businesspeople who sought government favors to provide them with advantages against competitors that would have been impossible in a totally free market. (Businesspeople have often been anything but enthusiasts for true laissez-faire.) And there were other injustices reflecting inconsistency in protecting individual rights: the toleration of slavery (until the Civil War) and legal discrimination against women. But in the brief period of a century and a half, the United States created a level of freedom, of progress, of achievement, of wealth, and of physical comfort unmatched and unequaled by the total sum of mankind's development up to that time.

To the extent that various other countries adopted capitalism, the rule of brute force vanished from people's lives. Capitalism abolished slavery and serfdom in all the civilized nations. "Western technology made slavery unnecessary; Western ideas made it intolerable," observes historian Bernard Lewis.* *Trade,* not violence, became the ruling principle of human relationships. Intellectual and economic freedom rose and flourished together.

A system in which wealth and position were inherited or acquired by physical conquest or political favor was replaced by one in which rewards had to be earned by productive work. By closing the doors to force, capitalism threw them open to achievement. Rewards were tied to production, not to extortion; to ability, not to brutality; to the capacity for furthering life, not to that for inflicting death. For the first time in history, intelligence and enterprise had a broad social outlet— they had a market.

Much has been written about the harsh conditions of life during the early years of capitalism. When one considers the level of material existence from which capitalism raised people and the comparatively meager amount of wealth in the world when the Industrial Revolution began, what is startling is not the slowness with which capitalism liberated men and women from poverty, but the speed with which it did so.† Once individuals were free to act, ingenuity and inventiveness proceeded to raise the standard of living to heights that a century earlier would have been judged fantastic.

But there was a price. A free society does not imagine that it can abolish all risk and uncertainty from human existence. It

---

*"Eurocentrism Revisited," *Commentary,* December 1994.

†For example, with respect to the impact of the Industrial Revolution and capitalism in England, a 1983 study by Peter Lindert and Jeffrey Williamson found that the real wages of English blue-collar workers doubled between 1819 and 1851.

provides a context in which men and women can act, but it does not and cannot guarantee the results of any individual's efforts. What it asks of people is self-responsibility.

The desire for security is entirely reasonable if it is understood to mean the security achieved through the legal protection of one's rights and through one's own savings, long-range planning, and the like. But life is an intrinsically risky business, and uncertainty is inherent in our existence. No security can ever be absolute.

This is accepted more readily if you have a decent level of self-esteem—that is, if you have fundamental confidence in your ability to cope with life's challenges. But to the extent that self-esteem is lacking, then the self-responsibility that a free society requires can be terrifying. Instead, we may long for a guaranteed, Garden of Eden existence in which all our needs are met by others.

We can observe this attitude in the two main camps that opposed a free-market society in the nineteenth century: the medievalists and the socialists. Longing for some version of a resurrected feudal order, the medievalists dreamed of abolishing the Industrial Revolution. They found spiritually repugnant the disintegration of feudal aristocracy, the sudden appearance of fortune makers from backgrounds of poverty and obscurity, the emphasis on merit and productive ability, and above all the pursuit of profit. They longed for a return to a status society. "Commerce or business of any kind," wrote John Ruskin, "may be the invention of the devil." The socialists wished not to abolish the Industrial Revolution but to take it over—to retain the effects, material prosperity, while eliminating the cause, political and economic freedom. They cursed the "cold impersonality" of the marketplace and the "cruelty" of the law of supply and demand, and above all they cursed the pursuit of profit. They proposed to substitute the benevolence of a commissar.

In the writings of both, one can distinguish the longing for a society in which everyone's existence is automatically guaranteed—that is, in which no one bears responsibility for his or her existence and well-being. Both camps characterized their ideal society by freedom from rapid change or challenge, or from the exacting demands of competition. It was a society in which each must do his or her prescribed part to contribute to the well-being of the whole, but in which no one faced the necessity of making choices that crucially affected his or her life and future. It was a society in which the question of what you earned or did not earn did not come up, in which rewards were not related to achievement, and in which someone's benevolence assured that you never had to bear responsibility for the consequences of your errors. The sin of capitalism, in the eyes of its critics, was that it did not deliver this protection.

While capitalism offered spectacular improvements in the standard of living and undreamed-of opportunities for the ambitious and adventuresome, it did not offer relief from self-responsibility. It counted on it. It was a system geared to individuals who trusted themselves—trusted their minds and judgment—and who believed that the pursuit of achievement and happiness was their birthright. It was a system geared to self-esteem.

In the earlier years of our history, when people spoke of rights they meant either the natural rights described above or their derivatives, as spelled out in the Constitution and Bill of Rights. Or they meant contractually *acquired* rights, such as the right to take possession of a piece of property you have purchased. In the first two instances, the primary focus was on protecting the individual citizen *against the government*. Insofar as these rights pertained to relationships in the private sector, the sole obligation of people was to abstain from using force or fraud in their interactions with others. In the case of contractually acquired rights, the sole obligation was to honor your agreements and commitments. No great drain on the public treasury was required to secure such rights—nothing remotely approaching a third or half of one's income. The cost of a government performing this function was marginal. But in the twentieth century, a new notion of rights became fashionable that negated the earlier ones.

Ironically, it was the very success of the American system that made this development possible. As our society became wealthier, it began to be argued that people were "entitled" to all sorts of things that would have been unthinkable earlier. Eighty years ago, few would have suggested that everyone had a "right" to "adequate housing" or "the best available health care." It was understood that housing and health care were economic goods and, like all economic goods, had to be produced by someone. They were not free gifts of nature and did not exist in unlimited supply. Now, however, at the sight of our growing prosperity, intellectuals and politicians credited not freedom but *the government* with the new wealth. And they began to declare that government could do more than merely guarantee the protection of rights and establish a more or less level playing field, which was the original American idea but which now seemed too modest a goal. *Government could become an agency for achieving any social goal thought to be desirable.* In the growing enthusiasm for government regulation, planning, and expanded "services," especially since the nineteen-thirties, it was not a long step from "it would be desirable" to "people are entitled." *Desires* thus became *rights.*

For example if a man *wanted* to be a farmer, then under the philosophy of Roosevelt's New Deal the fact that his farm could not support itself need not be an impediment: Agricultural subsidies could make his desire attainable. Of course, to correct the "mistakes" of free-market capitalism, political coercion became necessary. For wealth to be "redistributed," first it must be created and then it must be expropriated. Citizens' taxes paid the farm subsidies. These subsidies had the effect of driving up the cost of farm products, for which again citizens paid. *Their* rights were expendable. Whenever artificial "rights" are enforced by a government, genuine rights inevitably are sacrificed.

To quote novelist-philosopher Ayn Rand in her essay on "Man's Rights" in *The Virtue of Selfishness:*

> Observe . . . the intellectual precision of the Founding Fathers: they spoke of the right to *the pursuit* of happiness—*not* of the right to happiness. It means that a man has the right to take the actions he deems necessary to achieve his happiness; it does *not* mean that others must make him happy.
>
> The right to life means that a man has the right to support his life by his own work . . . it does *not* mean that others must provide him with the necessities of life.
>
> The right to property means that a man has the right to take the economic actions necessary to earn property, to use it, and dispose of it; it does *not* mean that others must provide him with property.
>
> The right of free speech means that a man has the right to express his ideas without danger of suppression, interference or punitive action by the government. It does *not* mean that others must provide him with a lecture hall, a radio station or a printing press through which to express his ideas.
>
> Any undertaking that involves more than one man, requires the *voluntary* consent of every participant, but none has the right to force his decision on others.

Under pure capitalism—that is, a system based on the inviolability of individual rights—a farm that could not maintain itself in a free market could not remain in existence. Under an increasingly "mixed economy," the impossible became possible by transferring to others the burden of one's failures, which the government alone had the power to enforce. This particular program was introduced by a Democrat, but for a very long time it was hard to find a Republican politician—notwithstanding all the free-enterprise rhetoric—who would dare challenge the sacred cow of farm subsidies (or some other form of financial aid), since so many of these farmers are Republicans. As this is being written (February 1995) our agricultural policy is at last being called into question by some members of the new Republican majority, but the outcome cannot yet be predicted. Chances of a radical change seem unlikely.

This is not an essay on political economy, and I shall not attempt to retrace the steps by which this country moved from something close to laissez-faire to the extravagantly regulated system we have today. Nor will I attempt to address the many issues that would be essential if I were to attempt to argue for the libertarian vision of the good society. The defining principle of libertarianism is the abolition of the initiation of physical coercion from human relationships. (I say "initiation" because of course force may be justified in self-defense.) Libertarians advocate freedom of production and trade, freedom (to quote Robert Nozick) of capitalist acts between consenting adults. And on this subject, there is ample evidence—available to anyone who is willing to do the homework—that, apart from any question of its morality, government regulation of our economic activities *does not work*. As Peter Drucker observes in *The New Realities,* "The Chicago economist George J. Stigler (winner of the 1982 Nobel Prize in Economics) has shown in years of painstaking research that not one of the regulations through which the U.S. government has tried over the years to control, direct, or regulate the economy has succeeded. They were either ineffectual or they produced the opposite of the intended results." There are reasons for this, among them that the immoral is not practical, but that is outside the scope of this discussion. Here, we want to focus not on the mixed economy, but on the role the government has played in undermining respect for self-responsibility in our society—and in creating a nation of dependents who can no longer imagine a life without government support, involvement, and regulation.

Under a mixed economy, government intervention can take many forms, from restricting the freedom of producers in the name of protecting consumers, to granting some business group monopolistic powers that shield it from competitors, to special subsidies given to a privileged sector claiming to have unique needs, to the welfare programs that have been sweeping the country since the sixties in a protracted assault on the practice of self-responsibility in the name of compassion. But the essential pattern is always the same: the violation of the rights of some (or all) individuals in the name of allegedly serving the interests of a particular group.

I say "allegedly" because the welfare programs were intended to solve problems that have gotten steadily worse since the legislation was enacted. This is made devastatingly clear in such powerful critiques of our welfare system as Charles Murray's *Losing Ground*.

The world of government operates very differently from the world of business. In business, when millions of dollars are poured into a project that does not deliver on any of the promises of its advocates, the project is typically dropped and the judgment of its advocates is reassessed. Not having unlimited resources, business is obliged to pay attention to outcome. Failure is a signal to go back to the drawing board. In the world of welfare, entitlement programs, and "social engineering" overseen by bureaucrats with the business acumen of social workers, *outcome is less important than intentions*.

Never mind that crime is a national forest fire raging out of control and that actual crime statistics are demonstrably higher than official government figures.* Never mind that the underclass is expanding, not diminishing. Never mind that the most important economic gains made by African Americans all took place *before* President Lyndon Johnson's civil rights legislation, that many black leaders are now saying that the situation has *worsened* since, that government policies and programs have encouraged millions of people to think of themselves as helpless children for whom dependence on the state is a necessity. Never mind that our "humanitarian" tax laws and welfare system play a major role in the breakup of black families by financially penalizing a family that remains intact and rewarding one in which the husband departs. (The absence of a male figure in the household has been tied to young people's disposition to crime, teenage pregnancy, and drug addiction.) Never mind that the people the programs are designed to help are falling farther and farther behind. Never mind that our welfare/entitlement programs have created a nation of dependents and are threatening to bankrupt us. If our motive is compassion for the unfortunate, it seems we do not have to be concerned with whose rights are sacrificed to pay for it nor what kind of personal and social outcomes we produce.

The message of our welfare system is that we are not responsible for our lives and well-being. The message of our legal system is that we are not responsible for our actions. (Has getting away with murder ever been easier in a civilized society?) The message of our political leaders throughout most of this century is that if they are elected, ways can always be found to transfer the burden of our needs and our mistakes to someone else.

With regard to this last, it is the essence of a mixed economy. Such a system means *government by pressure groups,* a state

---

*For details, see *Criminal Justice?* mentioned earlier.

of affairs in which various gangs ("special interests") compete for control of the machinery of government to win legislation providing them with the particular favors or protections they seek, always justified, needless to say, by ritualistic references to "the common good." The Founding Fathers were keenly aware of this danger. In the *Federalist Papers,* No. 10, James Madison warned of the threat represented by special-interest groups when democracies are not limited by individual rights. Special-interest groups prevail, he cautioned, because the benefits they receive from the government are concentrated, while the costs they impose on the taxpayers are diffuse.

Our government has poured into regulatory agencies, welfare programs, and every imaginable kind of statist intervention into the lives of citizens trillions of dollars that in private hands could have been put to productive use. What we have to show for it is a society characterized by:

- Increasing polarization between every kind of social faction

- Massive, inarticulate rage and suspiciousness of anyone who does not share our opinions

- Widespread cynicism

- Escalating violence and crime of unprecedented magnitude

- Escalating conflict between the young and the elderly (provoked by our social security program among other things)

- Increasing conflict among various ethnic groups

- An underclass that keeps growing and growing, nurtured by intellectuals who advocate more of the poison that is killing them—the politics of victimology and entitlement

- A general deterioration in the quality of life

Government is not the sole cause of these problems, although its contribution has been enormous. *A fact avoided by our political world is that all the social evils government intervention was supposed to ameliorate have grown steadily worse in direct proportion to the degree of the intervention.*

Am I suggesting that no social group has improved its circumstances over the past half-dozen decades? Of course not. What I am saying is that government efforts were not responsible, despite the self-congratulatory propaganda to the contrary.

During the eighties, for example, women enjoyed historically unprecedented gains in wages, in entry into such traditionally male professions as business, law, and medicine, and in education. According to studies by three women economists reported in the *New York Times* by business writer Sylvia Nasar, in that one decade women made almost as much progress as in the preceding ninety years. Ms. Nasar writes: "Far from losing ground, women gained more in the 1980s than in the entire postwar era before that. And almost as much as between 1890 and 1980." This was principally due to economic forces that drew more and more women into the marketplace, and also to shifts in our values regarding women's role in the world. In other words, these gains were in the *voluntary* domain, not the *coercive* (political) domain.

West Indian blacks in the United States, who come from a background of intact families, respect for hard work, and an ethic of self-responsibility, have not typically looked to the government for special forms of political protection and favoritism. They take any work available, often beginning on the lowest levels, just to get started in the economy; they may begin on low levels, but they do not remain there. They rise as fast or faster than many whites. "Second-generation West Indians have higher incomes than whites," reports economist Thomas Sowell in his illuminating study, *Ethnic America*. Furthermore, he writes, "As of 1969 . . . [w]hile native blacks had an unemployment rate above the national average, West Indian blacks had an unemployment rate beneath the national average." They are a walking refutation of standard explanations of poverty among blacks primarily in terms of racial discrimination. They sometimes look with quiet scorn on those African Americans for whom their victimhood, helplessness, and necessary dependency are axioms, and who regard low-paying, menial jobs as beneath their dignity but do not regard welfare as beneath it. (It should also be said that there are many African Americans who share the West Indian perspective.) Both groups are black, but the difference in how far and how fast they rise is an issue of differences in their culture and *values*. A mind-set of self-responsibility is not a peripheral but a central issue here.

In the same book quoted above, Sowell describes the striking social and economic gains that native African Americans have made during this century, which have far more to do with individual initiative than with any government assistance. Then he goes on to observe:

> Along with general progress, blacks have experienced retrogression in particular areas. The proportion of one-parent, female-headed black families increased from 18 percent in 1950 to 33 percent in 1973—from double the white percentage in 1950 to more than triple the white percentage in 1973. Despite attempts to depict this as a "legacy of slavery," one-parent, female-headed black families were a rare phenomenon in earlier times, even under slavery. The proportion of blacks on welfare also rose during the 1960s and 1970s, as the proportion in poverty declined. The pro-

portion of the black population that is working has been declining both absolutely and relative to whites. Unemployment among blacks has risen, also absolutely and relative to whites. Black teenage unemployment in 1978 was more than five times what it had been thirty years earlier. Among the factors responsible, a number of government programs—notably the minimum wage laws—have made it more difficult for blacks to find jobs, and other government programs—notably welfare—have made it less necessary.

I am aware that the social issues I touch on in this section are complex, many-faceted, and difficult to address briefly. I am also aware that my particular perspective is radical. It does not challenge "welfare as we know it" (almost everyone agrees our present system is a mess). It does not advocate reform. *It challenges the underlying principle of welfare itself.* By this I mean the doctrine that some people have an unearned claim on the mind, energy, and effort of others who have no choice in the matter. This doctrine treats people not as ends in themselves but as means to the ends of others, and asserts the moral right to do so.

No, I am not advocating the termination of all welfare programs overnight. They need to be phased out over time and with other political corrections to minimize the stress of transition to a truly free society. That, at any rate, is what I would be arguing were this a book about political philosophy rather than a book about self-responsibility.

Here, I can only hint at the libertarian perspective, with no time or space to clarify and amplify it, let alone answer the dozens of challenging questions that a reasonable person could be expected to raise. My purpose in doing so is to drive home the idea that whatever merits we ascribe to our present system, we cannot maintain that that system supports independence or self-reliance. Many of us have talked to young, unwed mothers (white and black) whose attitude is "Why *shouldn't* I have another child? The government will take care of us." We have talked to men and women (white and black) who say "Why *should* I struggle to get a job when I can get a government check?" Who taught them to think this way?*

As to those who are genuinely in trouble and not merely cashing in on the philosophy of entitlement, do I believe it a proper human goal to alleviate suffering and offer a helping hand? Of course. How can one not? There are, however, many things I am in favor of that I do not see as proper functions of a government. Charity is one of them. The question is not whether one believes in benevolence and mutual aid. The question is whether one thinks in terms of voluntary choice or governmental coercion. Kindness is a virtue, to be sure. But it is not grounds for sacrificing individual rights. Nothing is. And it is one of the many intellectual ironies and disgraces of our age that those who protest coercion are called "cruel" and "reactionary" while those who embrace it are called "compassionate" and "progressive."

There is nothing compassionate or progressive about imposing one's values on others at the point of a gun. And that, ultimately, is what we are talking about, however it is rationalized and dressed up to sound "liberal" and "enlightened."

The ideal of self-responsibility in no way forbids us to help one another, within limits, in times of need. As noted earlier, Americans have a long tradition of doing this. We are the most charitable people in the world. This is not a contradiction but

---

*For an important part of the answer, see *The Dream and the Nightmare: The Sixties' Legacy to the Underclass,* by Myron Magnet. In this remarkable work of social analysis, the author presents evidence that the rebellion of the sixties against an ethic of hard work, self-discipline, and deferred gratification—in the name of "I want it now and without effort!"—generated a shift of values that was internalized by the underclass more than by any other group, with tragic, demoralizing results. Government social policy was not the cause of this culture shift but an expression of it.

a natural result of the fact that ours is the first and still the only country in history to proclaim the right to selfishness in "the pursuit of happiness." The happiness the Declaration of Independence refers to is our own. In proclaiming and defending our right to pursue our own self-interest, *to live for our own sake,* the American system released the innate generosity in everyone (when they are not treated as objects of sacrifice). It is interesting to observe that during the eighties, the so-called "decade of greed," Americans gave more than twice the amount to charity that they had given in the previous decade, in spite of changes in the tax laws that made giving less advantageous. Our private, not-for-profit organizations—the Boy Scouts and Girl Scouts, the Salvation Army, churches, not-for-profit hospitals, and philanthropic agencies of every conceivable kind—perform benevolent work far more extensive than in any other country. In Europe, if such services exist, they are part of the political, coercive apparatus rather than the private, voluntary realm. Alexis de Tocqueville observed in 1831 that our voluntary spirit is what makes us different from Europeans. Americans have a long and impressive record of developing private and noncoercive solutions to social needs, and we must cultivate and build on this tradition.*

What needs to be challenged in our country today is not the desirability of helping people in difficulty (intelligently and without self-sacrifice), but rather the belief that it is permissible to abrogate individual rights to achieve our social goals. We must stop looking for some new use of force every time we en-

---

*For an interesting discussion of the growing importance of this "third sector" in the American economy—that is, the not-for-profit institutions aimed at addressing a variety of human needs, and doing so far more effectively than any government—see Peter Drucker's *The New Realities.* For discussion of why charitable and philanthropic activities expanded so much during the 1980s (and why they may drop again under the Clinton presidency), see Charles Murray's essay "Little Platoons" in the anthology *Good Order,* edited by Brad Miner.

counter something that upsets us or arouses our pity.

As a first step toward a freer society, by stimulating new thinking about the best ways to solve social problems, here is one concrete suggestion. Let us bring the paying-attention-to-outcomes philosophy of the business world to our legislative practices. First, every piece of legislation and every government agency must spell out what it aims to accomplish and in what time frame. Next, it must be monitored periodically, and the public must be informed concerning its progress, or lack of progress, toward its goal. When the time set for the accomplishment of specific goals is up, the legislation or agency must go on trial for its life just as in business. It must not be allowed to remain in force merely because it exists. It must demonstrate results, and if it has failed in what it promised to deliver, *it should be abolished.* This policy alone will not lead us to a fully free society, and you do not have to be an unreserved advocate of laissez-faire to appreciate its merits. What it will do is raise public consciousness concerning the workings of our present system and perhaps introduce some element of accountability. As matters stand now, once a political institution is in place, it is notoriously difficult to get rid of, even when almost everyone agrees it is a disaster.

We heard a great deal about the need for "a greater sense of community." Government by pressure group inevitably polarizes; it is the antagonist of community. When people are fighting one another for the privilege of imposing their particular agenda by law, is it surprising that their stance to others is adversarial? Government by pressure group places farmers against city dwellers, the young against the elderly, women against men, the less intelligent against the more intelligent, the subsidized or protected industries against the unsubsidized or unprotected, consumers against producers, and the poor against everyone.

When people are fighting for special legal protection and privilege because "I'm more of a victim than you'll ever be," when no one is responsible for anything, and problems are always someone else's fault, is it reasonable to expect a flourishing of brotherly and sisterly love? Clearly not.

This is why I stress that individualism and self-responsibility are the necessary foundation for true community. If we are free of each other, we can approach each other with goodwill. We do not have to be afraid. We do not have to view each other as potential objects of sacrifice, nor view ourselves as potential meals on someone else's plate. If we live in a culture that upholds the principle that we are responsible for our actions and the fulfillment of our desires, and if coercion is not an option in the furtherance of our aims, then we have the best possible context for the triumph of community, benevolence, and mutual esteem.

Are there now and will there continue to be severe social problems challenging our resourcefulness, inventiveness, and ingenuity? Yes. Will other people sometimes make value choices we can neither agree with nor admire? Inevitably. That is the nature of life. But a culture of self-responsibility is not the best chance we have to create a decent world. It is the only chance.

There are many reasons why people have difficulty even thinking about the possibility of the kind of society I am projecting. Social metaphysics is one of these reasons. I am propounding an idea totally outside the mainstream of "received wisdom." There are no famous "authorities" to sanction it. There is no widely esteemed group in our culture with which such an idea is identified. It is certainly not "conservatism." It has nothing to support it except—I am convinced—objective reality.

Let me give an example that might help to make my perspective clearer. Imagine if since the start of this country we believed that it was a function of government to provide citizens with shoes, since no one could hope to have a decent life without shoes. Now imagine that in the nineteen-nineties a radical (meaning, in this context, consistent) advocate of laissez-faire capitalism were to suggest that shoes should be treated like any other economic good—that is, should be manufactured and sold on the free market without governmental involvement. "Are you *crazy?*" most people might say. "Do you want to see the poor going around shoeless? Have you no *compassion?*" And yet in our country people do not walk around shoeless, and the shoe industry has done an admirable job of making shoes available to the general public at reasonable prices. To be sure, there are shoes that sell for under ten dollars and others that sell for over eight hundred dollars, but I do not know that anyone sees this as a great problem requiring government regulation of the shoe industry. However, in my imaginary scenario, it might take a great leap of intellectual independence for a person to grasp how a privatized shoe industry would operate, especially with every influential authority condemning the idea as "barbaric," "retrogressive," and "inhumane."

Today, only a handful of people can grasp how a society based *consistently* on the principle of individual rights might operate, or to project how men and women voluntarily and on their own initiative might develop means to cope with the unsolved problems of our society. It will be a major step forward when more people are willing and able even to *think about* such a possibility.

Individualism

The idea of individualism is threaded through this book without explicit discussion. Let me say a few concluding words about it now.

In his challenging book, *In Defense of Elitism,* William A. Henry III makes this observation:

> The rest of the world wants to come here because America is better—not just economically better but po-

litically better, intellectually better, culturally better. Our
is a superior culture, and it is so precisely because of its
individualism. More than any other world power, in fact,
we gave to global consciousness the very idea of the individual as the focal point of social relations—not the
king, not the army, not the church, and not the tribe. Just
when the world is rushing toward us and our ways, let us
not slide toward embracing theirs.*

Individualism is an ethical-political concept and also an eth-
ical-psychological one. In the ethical-political sphere, it upholds the principle of individual rights. It insists that a human
being is an end in him- or herself, not a means to the ends of
others. It rejects the doctrine that we are born to serve others
and that self-sacrifice is the ultimate virtue. It regards not self-
sacrifice but self-realization and self-fulfillment as the moral
goal of life. It celebrates the human *person*. In the ethical-psy-
chological sphere, it holds that a person should learn to think
and judge independently, valuing nothing higher than the sovereignty of his or her own mind, and insists that any other
course betrays our well-being and our highest potential. Individualism is not solipsism, and it does not deny the importance
of human relationships or how much we learn from each
other or the fact that we can realize ourselves only in a social
context. It does not stand against community but insists that
independence is its proper base. It celebrates *autonomy*.

Just as a community is best nourished by the individualism
of its members, so individualism requires the foundation of
self-responsibility. It cannot exist without it.

If we understand this, we understand the inappropriateness

---

*Perhaps it is of some interest to mention that this Pulitzer Prize–winning
culture critic for *Time* magazine, and extraordinarily astute social observer,
was (he is deceased) not a libertarian but "a registered Democrat, and a
card-carrying member of the ACLU."

of attacking individualism by equating it with "doing whatever one likes." To do whatever I "like," regardless of reality, context, or the rights of others, and therefore regardless of my promises and commitments, is sometimes to use others as means to my ends and thereby to violate the very essence of individualism. An individualist lives by his or her own thought and effort, neither sacrificing self to others nor others to self. An individualist deals with others through the exchange of *values* (material or spiritual). This is what independence *means* in human relationships.

The notion of an "individualist" who respects no one's rights but his own is a straw man. If individualism is upheld as a moral principle, then it must be universal, must apply to *all* human beings. If I claim rights for myself that are inherent in my nature, I cannot deny them to you. If I deny the rights of others, I cannot claim them for myself. No one can claim the moral right to a contradiction.

Allow me a very personal example. When I was twelve or thirteen, I stole some money from the cash register in my father's clothing store. Everyone in the family was dumbfounded and no one quite knew what to say to me. The exception was my oldest sister, Florence, who was wise enough to know the words that could reach me. She knew that I already prized independence as a cardinal value. She took me aside and said, "Apart from the fact that you had no right to take money that didn't belong to you, stealing contradicts everything you say you admire. You talk about independence, but no one can be independent who takes what belongs to someone else. Doing so ties you to others in the worst way. Stealing is dependency. A truly independent person respects the rights of others, no matter what." That conversation happened over fifty years ago, and I am still grateful for it. It was one of the most important things anyone ever said to me.

Now let me share another story, this time about a corporate client of mine, to dispel another confusion about individualism. I was working with a brilliant founder-owner of a small but rapidly growing business who had difficulty understanding the idea of "teamwork" as it applied to him, although he had no trouble understanding how it applied to others in his organization. His staff complained that he often held himself aloof, failed to share information about his activities that would make their own work more meaningful and productive, and generally tended to operate like "the Lone Ranger," sometimes leaving chaos behind him. We discussed the need for a better flow of information between him and his people, and the need to break down the wall that was felt between him and them. He looked at me sheepishly and said, "I know you're right. I know it—in my head. But . . . all my life I've been this somewhat alienated character. You know what I mean. My people are right: I *do* see myself as the Lone Ranger. And boy! it's hard to let go of that."

I was silent for a moment, not certain how best to proceed, and then I remembered that the sport he most enjoyed watching was hockey. "Hockey is an interesting sport," I began—and he immediately responded, "Yeah, it sure is, I love it!" I went on, "Well, the thing about hockey players is, each one of them's a real individualist—they're anything but a bunch of conformists!—and yet, out on the rink when they're playing, they all absolutely count on each other, they *have to* be able to count on each other, and the more perfectly in sync they are, the more in tune with each other, the more powerful they are as a team. I mean, nobody does 'his own thing' regardless of what's going on around him. He does what the situation requires, right?"

He grinned and stared up at the ceiling, and I felt I could see the brain cells in his head whirling around purposefully. Then he replied, "Now that gives me something to think about, something that makes sense. Yeah, if I look at it that way . . . that's a kind of team player I can be. I can live with that." He reflected a moment longer, than repeated, "Yes. I can do that." Then he chuckled, "Hockey. Pretty good."

One last point: Individualism does not deny that we have responsibilities toward others, but it defines them differently from the way collectivism does. Individualism teaches that a person has the right to exist for his or her own sake. It views help to others as benevolence, not as duty, and as a choice, not a mortgage on our life that one was born with. Collectivism asserts that the individual exists to serve others. Collectivism rejects the entire notion of individual rights. It treats not the individual but the collective, the group, the tribe, as the primary moral unit to which the individual is subordinate, as we have seen in Nazi Germany, Soviet Russia, Red China, and other countries ruled by some variant of this ideology. Individualism holds that the primary responsibility one has toward others is to respect their rights and freedom, not to initiate force or fraud against them. Beyond that, we have the obligation to honor those agreements and commitments into which we have voluntarily entered. Finally, we must not be willing participants in a slave society.

But beyond that, are we our brother's keeper? Are we to justify our existence by the service we render others? Are we the property of whoever may be in need? As we have already seen, individualism answers *no:* Such bondage is incompatible with the principle that each person is an end in him- or herself and does not belong to others—the principle of self-ownership. This principle, to the extent that it has been implemented, is the crowning social innovation of Western civilization, the bedrock of political freedom.

The ironic thing about the ideas of individualism and self-responsibility is that everyone understands them properly and practices them appropriately *some of the time.* The question is, Can we learn to live them consistently?

Our answer to that question will determine the kind of world we create in the twenty-first century.

Appendix

A Sentence-Completion Program for Growing in Self-Responsibility

Throughout this book, I have given various examples of how sentence completion can be used to facilitate self-understanding and personal growth. In the program that follows, the purpose is to assist the individual's progress toward greater independence and autonomy. While it is designed to be of particular value to anyone struggling with issues of social metaphysics, it is by no means confined to that problem and can be used profitably by virtually anyone as a tool of self-exploration and personal development. As the title conveys, its primary goal is to facilitate increased self-responsibility.

Many other applications of the technique, some discussion of the thinking behind it, and other stems for other purposes may be found in my book, *The Art of Self-Discovery*.

The essence of the sentence-completion procedure, as we use it here, is to write an incomplete sentence, a sentence stem, and to keep adding different endings, *between six and ten*, with the sole requirement being that each ending be a grammatical completion of the sentence.

Work as rapidly as possible, no pauses to "think," inventing if you get stuck, without worrying if any particular ending is true, reasonable, or significant. *Any* ending is fine: *Just keep going.*

The art of doing sentence completion well is to maintain a high level of mental focus combined with a complete lack of internal censorship. Doing sentence completion on a daily basis as described here is a kind of psychological discipline, a spiritual practice, even, that over time achieves insight, integration, and spontaneous behavior change. People sometimes ask, "How do I integrate the things I am learning in sentence completion?" The answer is that practice itself, done repetitively, brings about the integration. The speed of your progress depends in part on the level of focus and consciousness you bring to the work both while doing it and later when reviewing and reflecting on your endings.

When doing written, rather than oral, sentence-completion work, you can use a notebook, typewriter, or computer.

WEEK I

First thing in the morning, before proceeding to the day's business, sit down and write the following stem:

Self-responsibility to me means—

Then, as rapidly as possible without pausing for reflection, write as many endings for that sentence as you can in two or three minutes (*never less than six, and ten is enough*). Do not worry if your endings are literally true or make sense or are "profound." Write *anything*, but write *something*.

Then, go on to the next stem:

Independence to me means—

Then:

Thinking for myself means—

Then:

Trusting my own mind means—

When you are finished, proceed with your day's business.

Do this exercise every day, Monday through Friday, for the first week, always before the start of the day's business.

Do not read what you wrote the day before. Naturally there will be many repetitions. But also, new endings are inevitable.

Sometime each weekend, reread what you have written for the week, reflect on it, and then write a minimum of six endings for this stem:

If any of what I wrote this week is true, it might be helpful if I—

Continue this practice on the weekend throughout the entire program.

When doing this work, the ideal is to empty your mind of any expectations concerning what will happen or what is "supposed" to happen. Do not impose any demands on the situation. Try to empty your mind of anticipations. Do the exercise, go about your day's activities, and merely notice any differences in how you feel or how you operate.

Remember: Your endings must be a grammatical completion of the sentence, and if your mind goes absolutely empty, *invent* an ending, but do not allow yourself to stop with the thought that you cannot do this exercise.

An average session should not take longer than ten minutes. If it takes much longer, you are "thinking" (rehearsing, calculating) too much.

WEEK 2

If I operate five percent more self-responsibly today—

If I think for myself today—

If I bring five percent more awareness to my deepest needs and wants—

If I bring five percent more awareness to what I truly think and feel—

I am becoming aware—

Don't forget the weekend assignment.

WEEK 3

If I am more straightforward about what I think and feel today—
If I operate five percent more self-assertively today—
If I treat my wants and needs with more respect today—
If I express myself calmly and with dignity today—
If I want to translate these ideas into action—

WEEK 4

If I pay more attention to my inner signals today—
If I am more truthful in my dealings with people today—
If I am five percent more self-accepting today—
If I am self-accepting even when I make mistakes—
If these ideas start working in my subconscious mind—

WEEK 5

If I disown what I am thinking and feeling—
If I place other people's thoughts above my own—
When I look at what I do to impress people—
If I fake who I am to make myself "likable"—
I am beginning to suspect—
Don't forget your weekend assignment.

WEEK 6

If I am more accepting of my feelings today—
If I deny and disown my feelings—
If I am more accepting of my thoughts—
If I deny and disown my thoughts—
I am becoming aware—

Week 7

If I am more accepting of my fears—
If I deny and disown my fears—
If I am more accepting of my pain—
If I deny and disown my pain—
Right now it seems obvious that—

Week 8

If I am more accepting of my desire to be liked—
If I deny and disown my desire to be liked—
If I learn to manage my desire for approval—
If I can acknowledge my desire for approval without being controlled by it—
If I want to translate these ideas into action—
Don't forget your weekend assignment.

Week 9

If I am more accepting of my deepest self—
If I deny and disown my deepest self—
If I am more accepting of my intelligence—
If I deny and disown my intelligence—
If I allow myself understand what I am writing—

Week 10

If I am more accepting of my thoughts and feelings, whether or not anyone shares them—
If I deny and disown thoughts and feelings others do not share—
If I betray my thoughts and feelings in action—
If I honor my thoughts and feelings in action—
I am beginning to suspect—

WEEK 11

If I imagine being more self-responsible—
If I imagine being more independent—
If I imagine looking at things through my own eyes—
If I take five percent more responsibility for the ideas I live by—
If these ideas start working in my subconscious mind—

WEEK 12

If I honor my judgment today—
Sometimes I keep myself passive when I—
Sometimes I make myself helpless when I—
If I pretend to be less than I am—
If I allow myself to absorb what I am writing—

WEEK 13

If I bring five percent more integrity into my relation-ships—
If I take five percent more responsibility for my choice of companions—
If I take five percent more responsibility for my personal happiness—
I take five percent more responsibility for the level of my self-esteem—
I am becoming aware—
Don't forget your weekend assignment.

WEEK 14

If I lived five percent more authentically today—
If I treat my thoughts and feelings with respect today—
If I experiment with being more self-assertive today—

If I am willing to see what I see and know what I know—
If I fully face the meaning of what I am writing—

WEEK 15

If I hold myself accountable for my promises and commitments—
If stop all excuse-making and alibiing—
If I refuse to surrender to helplessness—
If I were willing to say "yes" when I want to say "yes" and "no" when I want to say "no"—
I am beginning to suspect—

WEEK 16

If I were willing to let people see who I am—
If I took more responsibility for delivering on my commitments—
If I operate five percent more self-responsibly at work—
If I operate five percent more self-responsibly in my relationships—
If I choose to translate these ideas into action—

WEEK 17

If I stay connected with what I truly think and feel—
If I take more responsibility for fulfilling my wants—
If I refuse to blame anyone—
If I make my happiness a conscious goal—
Right now it seems clear—

WEEK 18

If I look people in the eyes and tell the truth today—
If I refuse to be ruled by fear of disapproval—

If I refuse to hide who I am—
If I am simple, honest, and straightforward today—
If I allow what I am writing to fully penetrate—
Don't forget your weekend assignment.

WEEK 19

If I bring five percent more integrity to my relationships—
If I remain loyal to the values I believe are right—
If I refuse to live by values I do not respect—
If I treat my self-respect as a high priority—
I am becoming aware—

WEEK 20

If I accept responsibility for my life and well-being—
If I accept responsibility for my choices and decisions—
If I accept responsibility for my actions—
If I accept responsibility for how I deal with people—
If I choose to translate these ideas into action—

WEEK 21

If I want to grow in independence, I will need to—
If I want to grow in self-esteem, I will need to—
If I want to be more authentic, I will need to—
If I want to outgrow dependency, I will need to—
If I am willing to experiment with these ideas in action—

WEEK 22

If I look at things through my own eyes today—
If I am willing to see what I see and know what I know—
If I am truthful today, even if it's difficult—

I grow in self-respect when I—
I am becoming aware—

WEEK 23

If I operate five percent more self-responsibly today—
If I operate five percent more self-assertively today—
If I operate five percent more authentically today—
If I operate five percent more honestly today—
Right now it seems clear that—

WEEK 24

As I grow in self-responsibility—
As I grow in independence—
As I learn to say what I truly think and feel—
As I learn to look at things through my own eyes—
If these ideas start working in my subconscious mind—

WEEK 25

Sometimes when I am afraid of self-responsibility I—
Sometimes when I am afraid of independence I—
If I want to outgrow any fear I have of self-responsibility—
If I want to outgrow any fear I have of independence—
I am beginning to suspect—

WEEK 26

One of things I've been learning through this program is—
As I notice when I am being self-responsible and when I am
not fully—
As I notice when I am being authentic and when I am not
fully—

As I notice how I feel when I am honest—
I am becoming aware—

WEEK 27

I feel most proud of myself when I—
I feel least proud of myself when I—
If I give myself credit for my willingness to struggle—
If I give myself credit for my dedication to personal growth—
If I allow myself to understand what I am writing—

WEEK 28

As I learn to translate what I am learning into action—
As I continue the struggle, even when it's difficult—
If I choose to persevere, no matter how long it takes—
One of the ways I am changing is—
I am beginning to suspect—

WEEK 29

As my understanding of self-responsibility deepens—
As my understanding of independence deepens—
As I learn to be more authentic when dealing with people—
As everything I am learning takes root in my subconscious mind—
I am becoming aware—

Week 30

As I learn to operate at a higher level of self-responsibility—
As I learn to operate at a higher level of independence—
As I learn to pay more attention to what I truly think and feel—
As I learn to treat myself with more respect—
As I go on translating these learnings into action—

When you complete this thirty-week program and want to carry the work further, I suggest that you go through the entire program again, from the beginning. It will be a new experience for you in many ways because, having gone through it once, your context has changed. You can do this program over and over, if you have the commitment to keep growing in this area.

If you would like to share with me your experiences of doing this program, I would be very glad to receive your feedback and observations. This will assist me in my own research, and perhaps I can be helpful to you. I can be reached at: P.O. 2609, Beverly Hills, California 90213. Phone: (310) 274-6361. Fax: (310) 271-6808. E-mail: 73117.607@compuserve.com.

Selected Bibliography

Bidinotto, Robert James, ed. *Criminal Justice?* Irvington-on-Hudson, N.Y.: The Foundation for Economic Education, Inc., 1994.

Branden, Nathaniel. *The Art of Self-Discovery*. New York: Bantam Books, 1993.

————. *The Disowned Self*. New York: Bantam Books, 1984.

————. *Honoring the Self: Self-Esteem and Personal Transformation*. New York: Bantam Books, 1985.

————. *How to Raise Your Self-Esteem*. New York: Bantam Books, 1987.

————. *The Psychology of Self-Esteem*. New York: Bantam Books, 1983.

————. *The Six Pillars of Self-Esteem*. New York: Bantam Books, 1994.

Connors, Roger, Tom Smith, and Craig Hickman. *The Oz Principle*. Englewood Cliffs, N.J.: Prentice Hall, 1994.

Dershowitz, Alan M. *The Abuse Excuse*. New York: Little, Brown & Company, 1994.

Drucker, Peter. *The New Realities.* New York: Harper & Row, 1989.

Farrell, Warren. *The Myth of Male Power: Why Men Are the Disposable Sex.* New York: Simon & Schuster, 1993.

Frankl, Victor. *Man's Search for Meaning: An Introduction to Logotherapy.* Boston: Beacon Press, 1992.

Henry, William A., III. *In Defense of Elitism.* New York: Doubleday & Co., Inc., 1994.

Lewis, Bernard. "Eurocentrism Revisited." *Commentary,* December 1994.

Magnet, Myron. *The Dream and the Nightmare: The Sixties' Legacy to the Underclass.* New York: William Morrow & Company, Inc., 1993.

Murray, Charles. "Little Platoons," in Brad Miner, ed. *Good Order: Right Answers to Contemporary Questions.* New York: Touchstone, 1995.

Myers, David G. *The Pursuit of Happiness: What Makes a Person Happy—and Why.* New York: William Morrow & Company, Inc., 1992.

Rand, Ayn. *The Virtue of Selfishness.* New York: NAL/Dutton, 1964.

Remley, Anne. "From Obedience to Independence." *Psychology Today,* October 1988.

Sowell, Thomas. *Ethnic America: A History.* New York: Basic Books, 1983.

Acknowledgments

I wish to express my appreciation to my editor, Marilyn Abraham, for the energy and enthusiasm she brought to this project, and for her many helpful suggestions.

Thanks also to Mary Ann Naples, Marilyn's successor, who saw this book through the final stages of publication and made me feel thoroughly at home with my new publisher, Simon & Schuster.

Thanks as always to my literary agent, Nat Sobel, for his unstinting support, dedication, and wise counsel.

And finally, my love and gratitude to my wife Devers for her excitement about the book, the stimulation of our discussions—and for the photograph she took that graces the front jacket.

Index

239

psychological dependence,
see social metaphysics
psychological determinism,
47–50, 53
psychological visibility, 68, 147
*Psychology of Romantic Love,
The* (Branden), 144
Psychology of Self-Esteem, The
(Branden), 44, 133
Psychology Today, 16*n*
psychosis, 24, 63, 81
as legal defense, 50–51
psychotherapy, 18, 19–21,
26–28, 30, 41, 54–56,
72–73, 95, 96, 98–105,
111–12, 115, 119–20,
125–43, 191–93, 219–20
acceptance vs. forgiveness
in, 137–39
blame and, 125, 126,
137–39
childhood history in,
125–26
choice in, 139–41
confronting the past in,
133–37
dependency and, 126–32
dissociation and, 133–34
emotional-release ori-
ented, 135
goals of, 26, 95, 126
hypnosis in, 127–28
integration in, 134
marriage and, 150–51,
156–58

process of recovery in, 134
"radical," 121–22
reality and, 129, 133–34,
138, 140
resistance in, 100–101,
134–35
self-responsibility and,
134–41, 142–43, 165–66
supportive of victimhood,
121–22, 132, 135–36,
141–43
tape-recording of, 128
see also sentence completion exercises
Pursuit of Happiness, The
(Myers), 9*n*

racism, 75, 106, 211
"radical" psychotherapy,
121–22
Rand, Ayn, 205
reality, 57, 63, 67, 72, 74, 97,
197
business organizations
and, 170, 171, 172
dissociation from, 98–99,
133–34
grandiose claims to cre-
ation of, 42–43
marriage and, 150, 163
psychotherapy and, 129,
133–34, 138, 140
in social metaphysics, 67,
68–69, 73, 74, 77, 78, 79,
80–81, 88–89

About the Author

With a Ph.D. in psychology and a background in philosophy, Nathaniel Branden is a practicing clinician in Los Angeles and, in addition, conducts business seminars, workshops, and conferences worldwide on the application of self-esteem principles and technology to the challenges of modern business. He is the author of many books, including *The Six Pillars of Self-Esteem* and *The Art of Living Consciously*.